Also in the Paragon House Writer's Series

HOW TO PREPARE YOUR MANUSCRIPT FOR A
PUBLISHER
David L. Carroll

A MANUAL OF WRITER'S TRICKS
David L. Carroll

GHOSTWRITING: HOW TO GET INTO THE BUSINESS
Eva Shaw

WRITING AND SELLING MAGAZINE ARTICLES
Eva Shaw

FORMATTING YOUR SCREENPLAY
Rich Reichman

WRITING
EFFECTIVE
SPEECHES

———

Henry Ehrlich

PARAGON HOUSE
New York

First edition, 1992

Published in the United States by
Paragon House
90 Fifth Avenue
New York, N.Y. 10011

Library of Congress Cataloging-in-Publication Data

Ehrlich, Henry
    Writing effective speeches / Henry Ehrlich. — 1st ed.
      p.   cm.—(Paragon House writer's series)
    Includes bibliographical references.
    ISBN 1–55778–484–1 : $8.95
    1. Speechwriting.   I. Title.   II. Series.
   PN4142.E37   1992
   808.5′1—dc20   91–28766
                                        CIP

Manufactured in the United States of America
10 9 8 7 6 5 4 3 2 1

For Sam, Mickey, Margie, and Tamara.

Contents

CONTENTS

Acknowledgments

I WOULD like to thank Becky Morris for the wonderful years of working together, her speechwriting archives, and for her speech files. I would also like to thank Jan Van Meter, Tim Koranda, Richard Sorensen, Ned Scharff, Jeff Schaire, April Klimley, and Peter Carey for sharing their material with me, and Tamara Glenny Ehrlich, for reading this stuff.

I gratefully acknowledge the members and associates of the Blackwood Group, and the many friends, colleagues, neighbors, and baby-sitters who have listened to most of the original commentary in this book over the years. Finally, many thanks to PJ Dempsey for buying the book and putting me back into print under my own name.

Introduction

AFTER ten years as a professional speechwriter, I have trouble writing a letter and signing my own name to it. Writing a book about speechwriting is hard, too. But I've got a few things to say about the subject, so I'll just pretend I'm someone else and write it for him.

Why Write Good Speeches?

One of the most valuable skills in any walk of life is to speak well. The ability to speak effectively pays off in everything from job interviews to being president of the United States, and there are whole shelves of books to help you learn how to do it.

There are fewer books on how to *write* a speech, and it's a good thing, too, as my publisher will attest. But the ability to write a speech is a tremendous advantage, because there aren't that many people who can do it well. And the better the material, whether it's for your own purposes or for someone else, the more memorable and effective it will be.

I have seen it over and over again. Good speeches, with a touch of humor, a touch of class, with a novel slant on a common subject or a commonsense slant on a novel subject, can make the difference between seizing and losing control of an industry agenda; between raising some money or lots of money for a good cause; between persuading people to act, or leaving them cold; between having them on their feet applauding or merely heading for the door; between nodding in agreement and nodding off.

This book is addressed primarily to people in business, as opposed to people in politics, for three reasons. One is that I write mostly for business people, so that's the area I know best. I asked one writer who has written extensively for both politicians and business people what the biggest difference is between the two. He said, "Politicians speak because they want to and business people speak because they have to. Politicians want their audience to carry them off on their shoulders, and business people just want to give the speech and get out."

The second is that I think business people probably need more help (and are usually willing to pay for it). And the third is that speechwriting is generally the same no matter who you are writing for. I once asked an Episcopal priest what the key to a good sermon was. He answered, "Always begin with a joke." If it's good enough for the church it ought to be good enough for the rest of us. Besides, I figure that if you're creative enough to write speeches to begin with, you'll have the wit to adapt most of this stuff to your own field—profit, nonprofit, or political.

I have tried to supply as much material as I can on the *other* partners in every speech you write—starting with the real author of the speech, the poor sucker who has to deliver it, as well as the people who have to listen. A big part of your job as writer of a speech is empathizing with all of them, however alien they seem.

I have tried to keep the style breezy, and full of illustrations (drawn mostly from the work of my friends and acquaintances) that help support my points, with quotations and anecdotes from here and there; much like the kind of speeches I like to write.

While some of what I say here has its roots in classical rhetoric, I don't think about Aristotle very much when I work. The style I use—and most of the advice and examples here will bear this out—is contemporary. It reflects what speakers can say convincingly and what audiences are likely to be receptive to. The old tools of oratory, including powerful projection and gestures geared to the unamplified ages of speaking as performance, don't make it nowadays. Television has changed the way we look at speakers, and with modern public address systems, a cooler style works better in live performance as well as on the tube. The frame of reference should conform to the cooler standards, too. Speeches seem phony when they give the impression that those who write them are more erudite than those who deliver them. So I try to anchor most of my advice within what are likely to be shared standards.

I hope you come away from reading this book alert to the range of possibilities you can explore, with the courage and enthusiasm to try things out. It pays to challenge your speakers and your audience—and at the very least it helps you stay awake.

(Note: Unfortunately, the overwhelming majority of speechmaking executives are still men, a subject I discuss in chapter 14. While I had originally intended to alternate between he and she when referring to speakers in the abstract, chapter by chapter, I realized that the overwhelming majority of real-life examples deal with men rather than women, so I am reluctantly bowing to the predominant facts of business life and treating the speaker as masculine.)

Section 1

GETTING TO KNOW YOUR CLIENT, AND YOURSELF

CHAPTER
1

Whose Speech Is It, Anyway?

1.1 Ehrlich's First Law of Speechwriting

When I was a very new speechwriter, I had to prepare some remarks for the chairman of a dinner who was raising money for cancer research by honoring a prominent athlete. I decided to combine the themes of cancer and sports by quoting one of the most prominent American sports figures ever to succumb to the dread disease: Vince Lombardi, legendary coach of the Green Bay Packers, who once said, "Winning isn't everything. It's the only thing." Surely this was a sentiment that could be applied as appropriately to cancer research as it could to football—probably more so. (Actually, it was another football coach, Red Sanders of Vanderbilt, who really said it, but I, and almost everyone else, was ignorant of that at the time. Besides, quoting "Red who?" would have raised more questions than it was worth.)

The event itself was the first opportunity I had ever had to hear a speech I had written. I sat up front, all ears. At least fifty people were sitting on the dais, and during the preliminaries all were introduced, including someone named Lombardi who worked for a sporting-goods company and who, I assumed, was a relative of the late coach.

Finally, my man rose and began to speak. When he got to the line about Lombardi, he decided to improvise. "Vince Lombardi, *whom you met earlier.* . . ."

I was mortified. The man had paid me good money to keep his foot out of his mouth and he insisted on putting it in anyway.

From that incident I formulated Ehrlich's first law of speechwriting.

If you're quoting someone who's dead, make it clear in the text that they are dead—e.g., "In the words of the late Abraham Lincoln. . . ." Well, maybe not him.

Luckily for my speaker, the Lord taketh away, but he also giveth. The public address system cut out at a propitious moment, and I was probably the only one in that well-oiled crowd who noticed the mistake. But it taught me a lesson about speechwriting that I think about in some way every time I sit down to put words in other people's mouths. Namely, that a speechwriter is not the author of the speech, the speaker is. The speaker must own the work. He can't say, like the third-rate actor who was booed during Hamlet's soliloquy, "Don't blame me. I didn't write this junk." If he or she insists on asserting that authorship by deviating from the text, the speechwriter has to be content to let it go, for better or worse.

Every rule has exceptions, of course. Henry Ford II left Yale without his degree because he hired someone else to write his thesis and was caught when the bill fell out of the pages onto the professor's desk. Years later, when he returned to the university to give a speech, he stumbled over a word and said, "I didn't write this one either."

I guess if you own the company, especially Ford, you can disown the speech, but in general, your speakers take your work as theirs, and therefore take it very seriously.

1.2 The Basics of Speechwriting

When you are writing a speech, you are writing for a live performance. You have to be prepared for acts of God, technical failures, and what passes in the realm of corporate and public affairs for artistic temperament. You've got to do the best job you can, assessing the audience, the occasion, the subject, and the speaker's strengths and weaknesses; finding the right material, the right line of thought, and the right voice; writing it, and then letting go.

1.3 Pity the Poor Speaker

Charles Gillett, former head of the New York Convention and Visitors Bureau, warms up an audience with the following joke: Nero (whose speeches were written by none other than the historian Seneca) went to the circus to take lunch with the Christians. The hungry beasts had their usual success until one fellow spoke to his lion, which listened and then padded away meekly. This was repeated several times, with several lions, each more ferocious than the last. Finally, Nero had the man brought to him and said, "If you'll tell me what you said to the lion, I'll let you go free."

The Christian said, "I told him, 'The winner of this contest has to stand up and say a few words.' "

Anyone who has ever had to get up in front of an audience can identify with the speaker in his plight. The one who has to get up and say a few words has the hardest job of all. The audience is judging him not just as a speaker but as a person and as a thinker. Imagine the embarrassment my speaker would have suffered if his exhumation of Vince Lombardi had come over loud and clear. In a room of a thousand or so men and women, he was probably the only guy who didn't know Lombardi was dead. Even without a speaker who takes liberties with the text, however, there are dozens of things that can go wrong, and probably will.

1.4 The Terror of the Blank Page—Why It's Hard for People to Write Their Own Speeches

Speaking is bad enough, and executives go to a great deal of trouble and expense to make it easier. A *New York Times* reporter has called speech training "the public equivalent of a root canal."

But if there's one thing as awful as what a speaker feels when he gets up to the microphone, it's the average person's fear when he sits down in front of a blank piece of paper. Writing your own speech is two of life's most anxiety-provoking experiences rolled into one. And that's where the speechwriter earns his keep. Most speakers would pay someone else to deliver their speeches if they could; getting someone else to write it for them is the next best thing.

And lucky for the professional speechwriter, because it's not a bad way to make a living. It's a bit like making up crossword puzzles and filling them in yourself, particularly if you can get interested in almost anything long enough to write a speech about it.

I realize that not all of you who are reading this book are professional writers. Some of you are general PR practitioners, while others may be staff people adept at crunching numbers, strategic planning, securities analysis, or some other discipline beyond my expertise. However, if your boss has asked you to write a speech, the problem is the same as for the professional. So for all practical purposes, treat yourself as a pro. And if you are writing your own speech, it might take some of the anxiety out of the process to treat yourself as someone else and have a little sympathy for him.

CHAPTER
2

The Speechwriter's Job

2.1 About Your Client

Speechwriting is a client-driven business. You're not the author. That nervous executive is. Few of us can just get up and talk. Mark Twain said, "It takes three weeks to prepare a good ad-lib speech." If it took Twain that long, think how hard it would be for your clients, or you, for that matter.

You can't look down on your clients for not writing their own speeches—or even, as is often the case, for not knowing what to say, let alone how to say it. They can do many things that you can't.

I tell people that my job is making extremely busy executives sound as clever and thoughtful as they would if they had time to do it themselves. It may not always be true, but it's a nice way of putting it that also allows you to suspend your own ego, while maintaining your respect for speaker, subject, and audience long enough to get the job done.

Others are less kind. Speechwriter Donald R. Nichols

told *Business Week*, "The people we write for don't mean half of what they say, but they say it because they heard someone else say it, and whoever that was got away with it."

I guess the half they do mean is enough for his clients.

There is certainly a school that says politicians want to become a sound bite on the evening news, while business speakers want people to forget they ever said anything. In fact, plenty of business people are so wary of being quoted or misquoted that they never speak in anything but platitudes and boilerplate. They're not much fun to write for. I once worked for a guy who felt that each word he said was scrutinized minutely and any deviation from a standard text would be studied for signs of shifts in a significant issue of the day. This is, I'm told, the way the Federal Reserve conducts itself, too. With an army of Fed watchers advising traders, clues to shifts in monetary policy can be worth millions of dollars. So good business sense makes for some of the dullest speechwriting. You end up going through and changing a few numbers and names, as if you were playing Mad Libs, a game in which the basic story is provided but players take turns filling in parts of speech.

2.2 The Growing Importance of the Speechwriter's Craft

Fortunately, most speakers don't want to be that dull. Speeches are an intrinsic part of any competent PR

9

strategy. Executives are devoting more and more of their time to communications. They want to use these occasions to make points about their business. At public events, they know that even if the local congressman isn't present, voters and campaign contributors will be. What they say will be taken seriously by much of their audience—and when people don't have strong opinions about issues, the first well-stated version will be the best remembered. Other opinions and ideas will have to supplant the first one.

Within companies, employees are hungry to hear what the company really has to say. A speech from the CEO is important to them. The thinking and wording will start to appear in speeches by lesser beings, company newsletters, the annual report, and the press. The better the primary document, the stronger these variations will be as well.

2.3 Getting to Know Your Client, if You Can

You frequently don't get to spend any time with your clients, which can be very irritating. There's a story, perhaps apocryphal, about a CEO who refused to look at any script until he walked up to the podium; afterwards he would call up the writer and deliver an abusive critique. One writer got his revenge when, having already secured a new job, he sent his speaker off with a script that said at the top of the fifth page, "Finish it yourself, you son of a bitch." The rest was blank.

Satisfying though this fantasy might sometimes be, the reverse situation is far more likely, one in which the speaker, or, more probably, a committee of subordinates, will weigh in endlessly with changes. Sometimes this will strengthen the speech; after all, they know the subject better than you do. On the other hand, it is just as likely that they will do their best to "dull it up" (in the words of Tim Koranda, whose work appears in these pages), i.e., correct it to the point where it loses most of whatever meaning you thought it had.

The Man in the Grey Flannel Suit, Sloan Wilson's classic novel of corporate life, has a nightmarish chapter in which the speechwriter, after initial encouragement from the CEO, sees his script homogenized to death by the chief's inner circle. No wonder he leaves the corporation, presumably to write novels, as Wilson himself did.

Chiefs of staff, accountants, lawyers—all have their own sensitivities, based on years of professional training and service, which they are paid to exercise when they read a speech draft. They also have their own prejudices, which they exercise, too. Someone will remember that in formal writing you don't use contractions, and will correct them all the way through till the speech is groaning under the weight of its own pompousness and is undeliverable by anyone but an elocution expert. Someone else, believing that "till" is an abbreviation of "until," instead of a good English word on its own, will change it throughout, upsetting your rhythm.

Others will say that you can't end a sentence with a preposition. Some will change *that* to *which* and *which* to

11

that, even if they don't know the difference between an independent and a dependent clause. What they don't acknowledge is that you are writing for the human voice, and that the speaker's better off if you strive to accommodate his natural speech patterns rather than try for an A in expository writing.

In general, it pays to have a close relationship with the client. But even a close relationship doesn't mean that the speaker trusts the writer's judgment implicitly and will take the work without revision.

2.4   Who Gets the Credit?

It's gratifying when you can say to yourself that you are the one who wrote the speech, although you will probably have to pat yourself on the back—no one else is likely to do it for you. Sometimes you may have to content yourself with even less credit. William Goldman, Academy Award–winning screenwriter, says that if the finished movie has the "spine" of the original script, the writer who gave it the spine can consider himself the author. Screenwriters at least get screen credit; you may have to settle for pride of spineship, too, but without seeing your name in print. *Speechwriter's Newsletter* bills itself as "the weekly voice of the silent profession." That sums it up pretty well. If you are desperate to "sign" a speech, you can occasionally slip in an original *bon mot* introduced by the phrase "as an associate of mine pointed out" or something like that, but only occasionally. Make sure that your appearance in the speech is motivated more by the message you want to get across than by the fact that you said it.

Remember that the final product frequently has very little to do with what was originally written. People who don't know any better think that the writer has only done his work well if a speech survives largely intact from first draft to delivery. The need for substantial revision may lower the speaker's esteem for the writer, and vice versa. But writing a speech is a collaboration. Don't forget the terror of the blank page. You are doing your work if you spare your speaker that discomfiting experience and give him ideas that catalyze what he really thinks about the subject. He may come back from the weekend with a product that bears no resemblance to what you gave him—or, indeed, no resemblance to what you thought he asked for—but you have done your job.

2.5 The Nature of a Collaboration

My friend Richard Sorensen has the enviable job of writing for Jim Manzi, the chairman of Lotus Development Corporation, one of the most interesting companies in the world. Manzi, a former journalist, has strong ideas about his work and has real conviction about the written and spoken word. Sorensen told me that it took time for him to "break the code" with Manzi, i.e., to pick up on the way he really thinks and speaks. From the outset of their work together Manzi was very patient and involved, and they developed a productive relationship.

A thoughtful speaker will value your contribution and acknowledge it. A speech doesn't have to emerge from your word processor as perfectly formed as an egg.

Be prepared for the committee. It's undignified, but it's also a fact of life. Lie back and think of the paycheck.

2.6   Speechwriting as a Job

So far I have attempted to put the corporate speechwriter's job in its place. You are part of an enterprise larger than yourself. If you are good at it, and recognized as such, you will extend its prestige and power. Occasionally, you will have somewhat greater influence. Some speechwriters are close personal advisers to their chairmen, sounding boards and devil's advocates with whom ideas are tried out, argued, refined, or scrapped. At other times, in the process of thinking through a problem, you will be the only one who sees it in its totality, and you can expose flaws in logic that can be corrected, saving the company time, headaches, and money. But the success of the corporation will be determined in places other than your cubicle. Most of the cash will go to others, along with the credit; that's just the way it is. Remember, Cyrano de Bergerac may have helped another man seduce the fair Roxane with the speeches he wrote for him, but Cyrano never got the girl himself.

14

Yet a certain amount of mystery surrounds speech-writers. You will find that people think you have the power to make policy and influence events. In politics this may be true. Memoirs by brains-trust types such as Clark Clifford have shown that issues of war and peace are hashed over within the speechwriting process. Hawks and doves fight for their language; and lives are lost or saved, depending on the result. But even little speeches can have substantial consequences. A former boss of mine, the late Will Sparks, wrote for Lyndon Johnson. Once he needed to flesh out a short ceremonial speech; in doing so, he proposed an initiative that, given the juggernaut legislative activism of the Johnson administration, soon became a government program. By the time he published his book *Who Spoke to the President Last?* in 1971, that program was costing the taxpayers $140 million a year.

If people want to believe that you have similar power in corporate writing, let them. It gives you more cachet at cocktail parties, although if you have the talents that go to make a good speechwriter, you ought to be pretty good at cocktail parties already (and if you write enough speeches, you will need those parties, or the cocktails anyway). The truth is considerably less glamorous.

2.7   Speechwriting Is a Craft, Not an Art

You supply the discipline; someone else supplies the vision. I have tried to put the writer in his deserved place, out of sight and out of any mind but his own. In the pages

15

to come I will talk more about how to best approach the process. I will give you hints, cues, suggestions, and examples that have worked for me and for others.

2.8   The Ring of Truth

Like a lot of the speeches they compose, speechwriters usually sound wiser than they are. In this book, the ideas contained in the illustrations are unimportant in themselves, so don't hold them up to deep scrutiny. Even if they're perfectly acceptable as ideas, that's not why they're here. Sometimes they are invented entirely for purposes of illustration and have never been spoken aloud. If they have the ring of truth, that's enough. That's the game. The ring is what you're getting paid for.

My late boss put it very succinctly in his book. He told of a young biologist who was interviewed for a teaching job in a Bible Belt school. Asked how he felt about the theory of evolution, the teacher said diplomatically, "I can teach it either way."

Sometimes you do indeed end up playing it both ways. When he was writing for the chairman of RCA, Tim Koranda wrote a speech warning against the dangers to the American economy of too many mergers and acquisitions. At the time, RCA was under siege from General Electric. When GE's takeover was successful, Tim had to write the same man's favorable announcement to RCA stockholders of the completed merger.

These events, and the speeches that went with them,

stemmed from business decisions beyond the power of the speechwriter to influence. Whether the merger was ultimately better or worse for GE and RCA stockholders will be decided by the stock market. However, it was certainly worse for Tim. GE has its own PR department, and the chairman's valedictory was the last speech Tim ever wrote for RCA.

Like any good adviser, you have the job of helping speakers arrive at the truth that's right for them, but in the end, it's up to them to supply the conviction that will make or break the company.

2.9 Helping Speakers Be True to Themselves

At times, executives have to give speeches that have nothing to do with their business. CEOs are apparently coming into fashion as college commencement speakers (at least in part, apparently, because they don't charge fees or expenses) and it seems that something comes over them when they speak to the young leaders of tomorrow. According to the *New York Times*, this results in a profusion of speeches saying, "Be true to yourself. Do the right thing. Make this a better world." From these speeches you get such memorable lines as, "Tomorrow is truly the first day of the rest of your life." And "America remains the best place on earth to live in and be a citizen of."

These speakers and their writers are selling themselves short. They don't have to pretend to be Father Flanagan or

17

Knute Rockne to be good role models. They are forgetting what makes them important. It's their insights,
gained through hard work and individual experience,
that make them worth listening to. They don't have to
brag, but they can at least arrive at the eternal verities by
a personal route.

Generally speaking, the speech will be more inspiring
and convincing if it deals with things that make sense
coming from the individual speaker.

2.10   Speechwriting as a Career

For me, the profession of speechwriting gained new
legitimacy a few years ago when my elder son, then six,
asked me, "Dad, who's Quasimodo?"

I answered that he was a guy in a book who rang the
bell in a big church in Paris. He asked, "You mean that
was his job?"

When I answered yes, he asked, "Why couldn't he get
a good job?" Like what, I asked.

"Like yours, writing speeches."

What does it take to be a good speechwriter? Speechwriters come from very different backgrounds. Some are
highly educated, with advanced degrees in literature,
history, and philosophy. Some have dabbled in politics;
some have done more than dabble. Some are mathemati-
cians. A lot are journalists.

Tim Koranda says, "Speechwriting is not an entry-level
position. You first have to learn about writing and the

world. Getting a shot at writing a speech usually occurs by accident. If you like what you're doing, you become a speechwriter."

I became a speechwriter by accident when some friends at a big PR firm asked me to do a speech over a holiday weekend; I needed the money worse than they needed to stay out of the sun.

2.11 The Matter of Money

Financially, the field looks bright. Jean Cardwell, a headhunter from Chicago, thinks that the day will come when corporate writers will earn really big bucks. She says that if million-dollar-a-year executives aren't satisfied with the quality of their speeches, they have only themselves to blame: if they're worth the million (and which of them would argue they're not?) then they ought to pay at least half that to find someone who can make them sound like it.

Currently, according to research by David Moyer of the search firm Fenwick Partners, a typical staff speechwriter is forty-one years old, has two degrees, sixteen years of experience in a combination of journalism, government, and business, and a salary of seventy-seven thousand dollars a year. Those who supervise others earn more.

Freelancers earn between fifteen hundred and five thousand dollars per speech, generally. If they are doing it under the auspices of a PR firm, the client is actually paying two-and-a-half times what the writer is getting.

19

Some freelancers have retainers of one hundred thousand dollars or more, based roughly on a figure of five thousand dollars for a twenty-minute speech, and with a couple of deals like that, their billings run twenty to thirty thousand dollars per month in peak season. Early fall is a big time, and again after Christmas, with many of the speeches delivered in warm-weather climates—very few conferences are held in Maine in the dead of winter.

Section 2

THINGS TO
LEARN
BEFORE YOU
WRITE

CHAPTER
3

What Makes a
Good Speech Good?

- A good speech depends for its effectiveness not only on the writing but also on the delivery, and on other things as well.
- A good speech is a persuasive speech. Persuasiveness results from a combination of factors, some rational and some not; the writer's control of them is limited.

A good speech can derive its power from information and logic, but if you rely on reason at the expense of rhetoric, you end up with a position paper instead of a speech. Audiences have a limited capacity to appreciate an intricately argued case or absorb vast quantities of information, so you should make your case by emotional means as much as by intellectual ones.

New York Governor Mario Cuomo's 1984 Democratic keynote address was a great speech. But was it a good one?

A year or two after it was given, Senator Bill Bradley of New Jersey appeared at a roast for the governor in Washington. He told the audience that sure, Mario was a great orator, but that didn't give him his due as a profound thinker. This was particularly important since Cuomo has publicly eschewed speechwriters, and writes his own. "To appreciate the depth of his ideas," the Senator said, "you have to hear them in the mouth of a bad speaker." No one in the Congress has a reputation for having more wooden delivery than Bradley, so he made a perfect guinea pig and proceeded to read the 1984 keynoter. It didn't take long for the assembled to start hooting and the point was duly made that a great speech isn't necessarily a great document.

Who your speaker is encompasses the qualities that make up the person you see, hear, and feel on the stage. *What* he or she is is what's on the résumé.

In the case of Mario Cuomo, you might say that he's effective because of who he is—the son of immigrants, a man steeped in history, the law, Catholicism, a fan and amateur scholar of Abraham Lincoln, as well as a man who's not afraid to pull the stops out on issues of social justice. He also has a powerful speaking voice, which he uses to great effect. As for writing his own speeches, the *New York Times* reported on June 3, 1986, that Cuomo once took a course from a priest at St. John's Prep in Queens, New York, in which the weekly assignment was to produce a three-hundred-word essay. It had to feature a word like *finger* or *drip* or *oops*. The kicker was that students couldn't use the verb *to be* in any form. After training like that, it's—oops—no wonder he likes to write his own stuff.

As for the senator from New Jersey, Bradley can't depend on who he is as much as what he is—a Princeton graduate, Rhodes scholar, the acknowledged Senate expert on the tax code and, for better or worse, the author of the greatest overhaul of the U.S. tax code in history. Of course, it doesn't hurt that he has been called the greatest college basketball player ever. There's something about having been to that particular mountaintop that makes us feel privileged to have him serving the public.

In business writing, you've got to grapple with what's likely to make your speaker most effective, and that will depend on more than information, logic, and ideas. You have to weigh those other elements—who and what the speakers are—in order to help them get the most out of what they say.

I know a chairman of a very large corporation who's very impressive as a speaker, yet he never uses a writer. Audiences go to see him because of what he is—a very powerful and influential man indeed—but he is persuasive because of who he is. He can get up and talk for almost any allotted period of time without referring to any notes. This is not a man with a gifted vocal instrument like Governor Cuomo's; his delivery is flat. But he is very widely read in history and economics, as well as the behavioral, natural, and applied sciences. His idiosyncratic way of looking at the world, gift for images and metaphors, and his often daring sense of humor are largely a product of his having looked at this very difficult material close up, in the language of scholars and laboratories, rather than through the filter of popular writers. At his best, this man forces his audiences to look at the world differently from the way they did before, and leaves them dazzled.

But if his audiences saw the transcripts, they wouldn't be persuaded at all. They almost wouldn't believe that what's on the page is the same as what they heard. The ideas are all there, but the logic can be illuminated only after an effort almost archaeological in its scope and care. As with Bruce Springsteen and Leonard Bernstein, if you missed the stage show, you can't fully appreciate the performance.

3.1   Illuminating Your Speaker

As a speechwriter, you are the intermediary between speaker and audience. You don't want your work to be accessible only after an editor gets through with it. You have to illuminate the speaker the first time around. To accomplish this, you have to know who and what your speaker is.

What did he study in college? Did he arrive at his current position by way of engineering, marketing, or accounting? These are self-evident questions. But go further. Is he also an amateur athlete? An elder in a church? An actor or musician? A parent? Identified with any special cause? Does he serve on boards, corporate and nonprofit, and if so, which ones?

Does your speaker have exceptional qualities? A good speaking voice? A good sense of humor? A compelling world view? If so, try to map it. If the speaker has a distinctive way of looking at the world, it's the best single attribute you've got to work with. If not, you may have to invent one.

What is your speaker? The CEO? Vice chairman? Head of financial control? Corporate treasurer? Head of marketing or quality control? A recognized industry expert? Is he a contender for the top spot at this company, or likely always to be second, third, or fourth fiddle? All the above factors count toward making your speaker credible, and therefore persuasive. They figure heavily in the choices that you, the writer, will have to make.

3.2 Getting the Message Across

When people ask me what makes a good annual report, I always answer, "Good earnings." All the vellum paper and four-color photography in the world aren't going to impress anyone if the bottom line is printed in red ink.

Likewise, in speechwriting, there's nothing like a strong message in which the facts and the philosophy are on the side of the angels.

It doesn't always happen that way. Pity the poor speechwriter who has to write a ringing case for the cigarette industry. (Maybe poor is the wrong word. Cigarette companies pay their PR people very well in order to get them to work for them.) But a lousy message never stopped a

27

good speechwriter. While the best medical case for cigarettes is that no one has ever caught cigarette smoke with a smoking gun, there are important issues involved that have nothing to do with smoking itself. The cigarette companies exploit the civil-liberties argument (remember Philip Morris's sponsorship of the Bill of Rights Bicentennial?) or focus on social justice: when governments look to excise, or "sin," taxes as a "painless" way to raise revenues, cigarette companies become advocates of the poor. And why not? Excise taxes are classic examples of regressive taxes, which fall most heavily on the finances of those people who can least afford them (and who, some argue, are least equipped psychologically to kick the habit).

The cigarette industry isn't the only one that has trouble admitting where its interests diverge from those of its customers. Many an ardent free marketeer becomes a protectionist when his own industry is under siege from foreign competition. Textile manufacturers who deserted the Northeast United States in the fifties and sixties in search of cheaper labor in the South—sound free-market business strategy—became protectionists in the seventies and eighties as imports flooded their markets. Oil men hate gasoline taxes because higher prices discourage people from driving, and they roll out the lobbying dollars when higher taxes are discussed in Congress. But if there's a threat of war in the Middle East, they order champagne with their windfall profits. They're not afraid of higher oil prices as long as they get the benefits of the increases, not the government.

Contradictions for big oil and gas don't end there. The industry is generically on the side of unregulated prices. They claim that free-market pricing will automatically bring supply and demand into equilibrium. But executives sometimes get pulled in two directions between industry bluster and market reality. A writer for a large company, whose work dutifully supported deregulation despite the fact that his company actually benefited from regulation, used to get memos from a senior exec suggesting that he "soften" his advocacy. "The point is," the writer says, "this guy wouldn't go to the chairman and tell him, 'Hey, you're all wet on natural gas.'"

A speechwriter has to be able to argue all sides of an issue because sooner or later, almost every company will get caught by the differences between its larger beliefs and its short-term interests.

3.3 You Have to Be Facile Politically as Well as Philosophically

While you may imagine that you're helping set company policy by enunciating it, you are in the thick of the battle between opposing forces for the mind and heart of that policy. Use all the weapons at your command— ideas, voice, and the identity of your speaker. Good speeches are a carefully crafted combination of reason and emotion; strong messages and strong speakers are uncommon luxuries.

29

CHAPTER
4

Know Your Audience

I once heard Senator Bart Gordon of Tennessee talk at a breakfast with members of the New York financial community. Like many politicians, and particularly Southerners, with their tradition of engaging, homespun rhetoric, Gordon is an accomplished speaker. That morning, he was in full command of his subject, he spoke without notes, and because he was a power on the Senate Rules Committee, the audience was fully prepared to take him seriously. All in all, a dream situation for a speaker.

He began with a joke about his early-morning jog, which that day had taken place in Central Park. He has no doubt used the same joke over and over again in his travels around the country, possibly changing the setting to the Chicago Loop, San Francisco's Golden Gate Park, and so on.

But on this particular morning it fell worse than flat. When he paused for what would normally have been a laugh, he met stony, dumbfounded silence. Anyone who had listened to his car radio on the way to the station, or watched the 6:30 news while getting dressed, or read a local paper would have known that the night before in Central Park, a young female investment banker had been beaten, raped, and left for dead in Central Park by assailant or assailants unknown. The senator had obviously been too busy jogging to catch the morning news.

The senator was clearly sandbagged by events; this is an extreme case of how a speaker can get caught out of sync with his audience. But hyperbole and extreme cases are a useful tool in rhetoric, and I chose this anecdote because I think the lessons of the incident are important to anyone writing a speech. You can't control events, but you must do everything you can to reduce the risks. The message is simple: Know your audience.

Knowing your audience isn't just a defensive maneuver, however. Chances are it will yield useful intelligence that, properly handled, will ingratiate you with your audience and help you make your message more persuasive.

4.1 Researching Your Audience

The obvious place to start is with the speech request itself. In some instances, your PR department, or a corporate subsidiary, may have arranged the date with a particular purpose in mind, in which case you can find out everything you need to know from the interested parties. In some companies, executive speech requests are handled by the department that writes the speeches, in which case the writer may be part of the process from beginning to end. Whether you opened the mail yourself, or took a call from the boss or an account executive, the method is pretty much the same.

The formal written request or invitation should state something about the objectives of the sponsoring body, whether it's a trade association, a company, a university, or anything else. Then skim through any program that may have been published in advance and read carefully the parts that pertain to the overall purposes of the event and descriptions of the organization (with, of course, particular attention to your speaker). Since it's probably too late to turn the speech down, try to figure out the advantages to your speaker of making such an appearance.

4.2   Questions to Ask Yourself

Who are the people in the audience going to be? If you are dealing with a manufacturing industry, they may be engineers, marketers, industry regulators, accountants, computer jocks, or any combination thereof. If financial, you may be talking to corporate treasurers, operations personnel, systems people, regulators, brokers, insurers, analysts, etc. Be sure that you don't exclude these people. They will take you more seriously if they feel that you've tried to gear your thinking to the issues they face in their specialties. Speech coaches tell their students that they cannot make eye contact with every member of an audience, but by shifting their focus to particular audience members for some length of time, they become more convincing to the audience as a whole. Attention to the particular in writing a speech does something similar. You may only be going the extra foot, but in the aggregate you gain the extra mile.

Who are the people on your side who know about the speech, and what do they know? Whether you are on the staff of your client firm, outside PR counsel, or a freelancer, someone should be available on your side to answer questions about the speech. These people will be especially useful in giving you a feel for the stake your speaker has in the speech, the politics of the appearance, and the audience.

Is a topic assigned? Don't feel bound by the description in the program or the speech title listed. Think about the message you want to convey. Such effective public figures as Dwight Eisenhower and Casey Stengel never felt obligated to answer questions on the terms in which they were asked. They spoke, but they didn't say anything they didn't want people to hear.

Does the conference have a theme? You want to figure out a special angle for your speaker. There's nothing worse than listening to a series of speakers who are mouthing the same commonplace wisdom on a subject, complete with the same latest jokes and facts. This can happen even if the conference organizers are carefully handing out topics.

Is your speaker kicking off or wrapping up the event? An opening speaker helps set the tone for an event. The closer has to summarize at some level, which is difficult if he hasn't been present the whole time. A closing speaker has to set an agenda for action. It requires a degree of vision.

Is he speaking at breakfast, lunch, or dinner? Speaking at mealtime is an honor. Make sure that the tone and content reflect it.

Is he part of a panel? The speech should be powerful enough to stand out in a crowd.

While you and your speaker are in charge of your larger message, all these things can, indeed should, influence the tenor of the remarks. The organizers or sponsors of the event should be willing to answer questions. You're doing them a favor. Don't be afraid to ask.

Read any literature handy, or go to the library and do more reading if you like. There are limits, though. Don't get too bogged down in formal research and ignore short-cuts that might be more effective. Call friends who may know something relevant about the organizations, the industry, the location. I once had to write for someone introducing Jeane Kirkpatrick, then the U.S. Ambassador to the United Nations. I found out from a friend prominent in neoconservative circles that she liked being referred to as "our man at the U.N." That line not only got some laughs, it made points with Kirkpatrick for the forethought it reflected.

This kind of research (not very time-consuming and often fun) will give you insights that no one else has.

*   *   *

Other kinds of information that will give you a big edge over other speakers:

The nature of the sponsoring organization. Will you be preaching to the converted? Will they be antagonistic? Does your speaker's organization have any history of conflict with them? Any industry is divided into factions. You have to consider whether your speaker's point of view will play with the grain or against it.

The location. Where is it and what should you know about it? There may be local themes and history that will lend themselves to discussion, e.g., sports teams, celebrities, ideas, inventions—anything that has brought the location national or international recognition. Show your hosts they're on the map and how much you appreciate it. On the other hand, there may be something going on in the area that you should know about in order to avoid it.

Don't come to New York and joke about crime. Johnny Carson used to get away with it—besides, he had to find some way to pay all that alimony—but the purpose of rhetoric is above all to persuade, and persuasion is based on sympathy as much as compelling information and logic.

Is the audience predominantly local, or are they gathered from all over? Local residents respond very well if they think you've taken pains to learn about them and where they live. It's their home; be respectful of it. On the other hand, if the gathering is mostly of tourists, any references to the locale should be pitched in terms of your shared visit.

What is the audience looking for from your speaker? Are

they in a position to buy something your speaker is selling? Do they want public or industry policy ideas? Do they want facts?

What are their sympathies likely to be? What are their fears and aspirations? This is a matter not of research but of imaginative speculation about the things you have learned. I once vetted a speech on business ethics written by a friend for a Wall Street executive. It was to be given to undergraduates in business administration at a large state university. It was my guess that in a business program at a big state school there was likely to be a large contingent of students in ROTC programs. Discussing unethical behavior in terms of, say, insider trading made sense from the speaker's point of view, since he came from Wall Street. But the harmful effects of such practices were somewhat abstract to most people, particularly in the prevailing atmosphere of the 1980s, when it was assumed that everyone cheated. It made sense to use examples that might have real immediacy for the audience, so I suggested that my friend write about defense contractors who cheat in their testing of new weapons systems. People who cheat in defense contracting business don't do it because they want weapons to be faulty. All things being equal, they'd like to cheat and still produce good ones. They cheat for business reasons. They have deadlines and budgets to meet. And they rationalize it by saying that the effect isn't likely to be any more harmful than insider trading. Unless . . . unless there's a war. In which case, their bum weapons could cost some of the students listening to the speech, and their friends, their lives.

Take the time to do the research. Sometimes the extra effort will pay off in material that makes the speech something special.

4.3 The Cheese Stands Alone—Or Is He Part of a Panel?

You have to consider whether your speaker is a solo act or part of a larger program. If he's speaking to the Town Hall of Orange County, California, he stands alone. The speech is the evening's entertainment. It will be broadcast and probably reprinted in a trade publication such as *Vital Speeches of the Day.* Your speech will become a primary document in the field. Other venues with similar prestige include the economic clubs of major industrial cities.

But it's very likely that your speaker is part of a larger agenda. This means that the material should be influenced by where it falls in the program. A keynote address sets the tone for the entire proceedings. With it, you have a chance to influence how the audience receives the whole event, or even establish the industry's agenda for a year, so be prepared to figure out what the key issues are and where your company should stand on them. Study the program with care and see what other people are going to talk about. Aim at getting the audience to hear the rest of the conference on your terms. The keynote is a special responsibility. As I've indicated, Governor Mario Cuomo of New York built a national reputation with his 1984 Democratic keynoter. But at the same convention four years later, Bill Clinton of Arkansas muffed his chance by prattling on and on. The critical consensus at the time was that it might take years and a lot of judicious editing before the party let him back on prime time.

If your speaker is part of a panel, you have to think beyond the text itself. I once had to write a speech for a banker who was appearing on a panel on interstate banking. The three other panelists all worked for institutions, including one in Florida, that were publicly identified with "regional interstate banking." This meant that they wanted to protect their institutions from having to compete with what they saw as predatory money-center banks by allowing mergers only with banks in contiguous states (except New York, Illinois, and California). My own client was prominently associated with the view that banks should be able to compete with others no matter where they were based.

I called the panel chairman and explained that my speaker was going to be Daniel in the lion's den unless he was allowed to lead off, and so define the terms of the debate. The point was duly made and the speaker gained the favored position. He made excellent use of his advantage. Noting the prominence of Florida bankers in the regional interstate banking movement, he compared the principle of regional banking to the behavior of certain "entrenched pizza interests" in Miami, which protected themselves by bombing new pizzerias, "lending new meaning to the term target market." The other panelists spent the rest of the presentation trying to deny any association with organized crime.

Speechwriting is a field full of such small problems, and such private satisfactions.

Section 3

WHAT THE AUDIENCE WANTS AND NEEDS

CHAPTER
5

Common Cause: Speaker,
Audience, Writer

An audience has a hard job. Not as hard as the speaker's, of course. Members of the audience can fidget. The speaker can't. Members of the audience can whisper to their neighbors. The speaker can't. But that's not why the audience is there. No one goes to hear a speech in order to ignore what's being said, to socialize, or to be rude.

Audiences are almost invariably receptive to their speakers. They don't drive to downtown Detroit in the middle of a snowstorm to make small talk over brandy and cigars.

In the triumvirate of speaker, writer, and audience, you, the speechwriter, are the only one who can draw any comfort from Mark Twain's words to a friend with podium fright: "Don't worry, they don't expect much." The danger for you is not public embarrassment or boredom, of course, it's that you may never work again, but don't let that bother you.

Of course you have high expectations, or you wouldn't

be reading this book. So pay attention to audience requirements as well as speaker requirements; ultimately,
they are yours, too.

5.1   How Long Is Long Enough?

William Henry Harrison's inaugural address in 1841
was nine thousand words long and took two hours to
deliver on a freezing March day. He came down with a
cold and died of pneumonia a month later.

If your speaker is going to go on for hours, he'd better
be a good speaker. Or you'd better be a very good writer.
Failing that, make sure the speaker is the dictator of a
country in a warm climate.

Someone once asked Abraham Lincoln how long a
man's legs should be. He answered, "Long enough to
reach the ground." A speech should be long enough to get
the job done, too. It doesn't have to be as long as Lincoln's
legs were. George Washington's first inaugural was 135
words long. Lincoln's Gettysburg Address was 265.

Obviously, one important point is how long the organizers of the event expect the speech to be. That's pretty
much out of your hands.

But whatever they tell you, do your best to cheat on the
short side. Listening to a good speech is easier than
writing or delivering one. Listening to a bad one is less
painful than writing one. But after a while, even a good
speech delivered to a good audience by a good speaker
will start to lose steam. Left to your own devices, try to

make a serious speech about twenty minutes long. That figure is a pretty good benchmark for everyone concerned—audience, speaker, and writer. You may need more time to make your point—by all means, take what you need—but give everyone, including yourself, a break. Don't necessarily write to the full allotted time. The moderator can always throw the floor open to questions unless your speaker doesn't want to answer them.

5.2 A Simple Breakdown of a Twenty-Minute Speech

Break your speech down as follows:

One minute of "throat clearing." This is a way of getting your speaker attuned to being up in front of his audience, acknowledging the occasion, the audience, the agenda, the time of day, and otherwise dealing with speaker's butterflies.

Two minutes of "joke." Make 'em laugh, if you can, with a joke, an anecdote, or quotation to rope them in, and launch your theme.

Fourteen minutes to make the meat of your argument with maybe three to four minutes on each of four key points.

Two to three minutes to sum up.

5.3 Your Master's Voice

You should capture the tone and diction of your speaker. This encompasses length of line, vocabulary, and sentence structure. Speakers are most at ease when they are speaking the familiar. Sentences and words that are too long and sentence structures that are too convoluted are hard for speakers to deal with unless they have a lot of rehearsal time, an unlikely event.

5.4   Keep Sentences Short

Actors train their apparatus for the stage. Executives don't. Give them a break. Long, complex sentences, especially without sufficient commas, are exhausting to read. When you're writing speeches you're not a writer, you're a speechwriter.

5.5   Be Careful with Long Words

Speakers can trip over them. Stage fright can tie the tongue of the most glib raconteur. I used the word *precipitous* in one of the first speeches I ever wrote. The speaker was a very smart man, a commanding conversationalist and, by reputation, a fierce negotiator who could browbeat finance ministers and central bankers all over the world. Yet he stumbled over the word. The next time I used *steep.*

When choosing a big fancy word or a simpler alternative, you have to consider the audience as well. In general, the same rules apply to them. Speak in words and images that they will understand without making them work too hard. You are trying to communicate a message, and your audience has enough to do without making them run to their mental dictionaries to figure out what you mean. A word like *precipitous* is often used interchangeably with *precipitate*. Don't make your listeners spend the next paragraph of the speech wondering whether you meant to say *steep* or *sudden*. When they are reading they have the luxury of thinking about the context, but not when they are listening. Use a ten-cent word like *steep* or *sudden* instead of the dollar alternatives.

5.6 Style

You are lucky. Stylistically, the same rules of thumb that make a speech easy for a speaker to speak will make it easier for an audience to digest. Strive for clarity, not complexity. Shorter declarative sentences. Unambiguous words.

CHAPTER
6

*Enriching the Language
of Your Speech*

6.1   Images and Metaphors

The same kind of individual care should go into choices of images and metaphors. They, too, should be characteristic of the person. When George Bush was running for president in 1988, his speechwriter became a celebrity. There have been celebrity speechwriters before: Mark Twain wrote for Ulysses S. Grant and Theodore Sorenson for John Kennedy. But I doubt that their work was identified as theirs almost as soon as it was out of the presidential mouth.

However, when you've got a candidate whose innate diction runs to "deep doo-doo" and "the vision thing," an image like "a thousand points of light" fits him like a petticoat. You start to look for the ghost. It's supposed to be a George Bush speech, not Peggy Noonan's new speech, performed by George Bush.

Still, that speech did what it was supposed to. People remember it, even if at the time it left them thinking

48

about who actually wrote it. Politicians are supposed to inspire. Statesmen are supposed to lead. Lofty rhetoric has a place in politics. It should produce an emotional response. There's such a thing as taking the oratory out of oration, and Bush's opponent in '88 did it. An acquaintance of mine was offered a crack at the Dukakis acceptance speech. Perhaps in the interest of favoring competence over ideology, a Dukakis theme, the candidate's aides told the writer he could do anything he wanted, as long as he avoided discussion of the issues and any hint of heightened language. Well, George Bush didn't need to be a thousand points ahead in the electoral vote against a candidate who thought like that, or whose advisers gave such instructions to his speechwriter.

6.2 Quotation, Paraphrase, and Theft

Plenty of people think that a good speech ought to be larded with quotations and references, and that the older the source, the better. The United States Government Printing Office has published a book of 2,100 quotes that have been researched at the behest of congressmen, attempting to the demand for quotations. Quotations can certainly put some pith into your speeches, but excessive quotation is a hindrance, not a help. You don't want them to wonder about whether the speaker actually read all the great books any more than you want them to think about the meaning of individual words.

I once asked a client, "Are there any authors you particularly like to quote in your speeches?"

"No," he said. "The only person who can get away with a lot of quotations is Walt Wriston, and I'm not sure even he can."

Well, Wriston, former chairman of Citicorp, can get away with it. If you read his collected speeches as published in *Risk and Other Four-Letter Words,* you'll find that they are riddled with quotations from and allusions to a breathtaking variety of sources in history, economics, literature, and philosophy. You'll also find that the citations are well integrated into the text and convincingly support Wriston's general thesis that markets ought to be unfettered by government regulation. That is itself an old message, dating back to Wriston's spiritual forebear Adam Smith, but in the sixties, seventies, and early eighties it had a fresh look to it that began to fray around the edges only after eight years of Reaganomics. People catch Wriston out sometimes, or raise a chuckle just by enumerating the quotes—making lists is fun—or they question whether the context is true to the author's intent. But the larger point is that you firmly believe Wriston has read the stuff he's quoting from. His father was a university president and adviser to U.S. presidents. Young Mr. Wriston grew up listening to high-minded dinner-table conversation, has kept company with statesmen and newsmakers for two generations and even his detractors admit that he was one of the most intelligent and influential executives of his age. He wears his erudition comfortably.

Nowadays, most executives can't carry it off. When they pad a text with a lot of quotes, you can almost see the price tag from *Bartlett's* sticking out of their collars. I remember the guest speaker at my own high school graduation. He hopped from one venerable idea to another, all of them in quotation marks. I kept thinking, well, it's nice the Greeks said all this stuff, but it was hard for me to believe that anyone could be that virtuous, let alone myself, or the speaker for that matter. He was so busy quoting other people that he didn't connect the dots, and so took all the timeliness out of all that timeless wisdom.

When you listen to one of those great-quotations speeches, you know just what Emerson meant when he said, "I hate quotations, just tell me what you know."

Practically speaking, there's also the fact that as speechwriter you frequently don't play as much of the part of arbiter of the speaker's mind as you feel you deserve. The higher up the speaker you are writing for, the more staff members will be contending for the status of intellectual gatekeeper, and they are generally suspicious of anyone who they think has read more than they have.

If it's any consolation, they often misjudge what their boss will accept, although you don't always discover the truth at the time. My friend Jeffrey Schaire, now editor in chief of *Art & Antiques* magazine, once wrote a speech for a banker and used a quotation from Marilyn Monroe in *Some Like It Hot* about how she always ended up with "the fuzzy end of the lollipop." When he took the speech to the PR person who hired him, the flack stopped short at

51

Marilyn and said, "That's got to go. This guy doesn't quote from anyone but generals or presidents."

Quoting from generals can backfire. Remember what I said about who your speaker is, who the audience is, and what the subject is. Consider, too, the person you are quoting from.

I came across this quote from General George S. Patton in a publication aimed at professional speechwriters: "No sane man is unafraid in battle, but discipline produces in him a form of vicarious courage." This comes across extremely wisely and well from Patton. He was physically courageous, brilliant, bred for soldiering, and a megalomaniac. The average corporate executive probably lacks all these credentials except perhaps the last. The quotation is cheapened when invoked in a discussion of corporate "downsizing," giving to United Way, or telling people they won't get a raise for eighteen months because the company's bond rating just went down.

Many speakers understand their limitations, so give them some credit. Years after the Jeff Schaire speech, I met the speaker and mentioned to him what his PR person had told Jeff. He said, "Gee, I'd much rather quote from Marilyn Monroe."

Every writer has his quotation stories. One tells of using a line from Machiavelli, only to have an executive ask, "Who is this guy?" (Another thing to consider: the quote survived the delivery, though the name didn't— the speaker stumbled over it despite rehearsal.)

Tim Koranda once used the J. K. Galbraith line, "In banking, tailoring substitutes for intelligence." It was changed in committee to "In banking, conformity is often valued over initiative." The thought's there, I guess, cut in tasteful gray flannel.

Remember, the choice of material generally means as much as the individual quotation. To give the impression that your speaker is the master of his own subject, draw the reference points from material that the speaker is likely to have read himself (or could have read if he weren't too busy).

6.3 Clichés

There are some quotations that everyone knows, and using them is all right, because when people listen to speeches, they like to hear familiar ideas and sentiments. They can digest them easily, like good strong declarative sentences. But you must use them correctly. The sign of an amateur is that he will use an old saw as if it were still fresh. Clichés can't be fresh, but they can be used in fresh ways.

A bad speechwriter will use a line like "As Calvin Coolidge said, 'The business of America is business.' That's as true today as it was sixty-five years ago."

A good writer will say, "Calvin Coolidge once said that the business of America is business. That was a long time ago. Today, the business of America is corporate raiding, white knights, golden parachutes, greenmail, and junk bonds."

A bad writer will say, "As Shakespeare wrote, 'Neither a

borrower nor a lender be.' Time has borne out the wisdom of those words."

A good writer will say, "When Polonius counseled Laertes, 'Neither a borrower nor a lender be,' those were the only alternatives. Had Shakespeare been writing today, he might have said neither an issuer nor an investor nor a leveraged capital specialist be."

A quotation doesn't have to be old to be exhausted. Yogi Berra's pronouncement "It ain't over till it's over" is still used as if it were the soul of simple wisdom. It isn't. But it's not dead either, provided it is used in a novel way.

If the quote fits, wear it, but give it a twist. The following was written for a non–Italian speaking American executive to be delivered to an audience of Italian Italians, to describe the precarious state of a certain industry:

> In the words of the eminent Italian-American Lawrence Peter Berra, "It ain't over till it's over." Or, as his Roman forebears might have put it, *nil desperandum.*

To use a line like this, you must assume that the speaker and the audience have a plausible grasp of Latin, and a taste for wry humor, so the approach will fit comfortably, as well as an appreciation of the oddball description of Yogi Berra. The Italian audience will appreciate the attempt to bridge American and Italian cultures, and probably most of them will recognize the Latin. A line like this will work only if elements like these are present.

6.4 Finding Good Quotations

Good quotations are a standard part of your repertoire, imparting historic and cultural plausibility, humor, irony, and good strong language.

One person I recommend against quoting is Will Rogers, who's the U.S. equivalent of Dr. Johnson. Oh, he's wonderful, wise, and funny, and a better writer than the rest of us put together, but when I hear his name, I picture the writer flipping through a book for just the right thing to say. If you're going to quote Rogers—or Dr. Johnson for that matter—attribute the words to a left-handed relief pitcher.

So where do you find the good ones? The Emerson line about quotations that I used before didn't come from *Bartlett's,* at least not for me. And I haven't read the collected works of Emerson, although I wish I had read more of him and a lot more of a lot of other authors.

In fact I got the line out of the *Wall Street Journal.* And therein lies the message. By all means use quotations to give your speeches color, weight, and variety. (Two other quotations cited in the same article are priceless, and as pertinent as the day's news. One was from Shaw, "A government that robs Peter to pay Paul can always depend on the support of Paul." The other was from a Russian observer of the U.S. Congress: "Congress is so strange. A man gets up to speak and says nothing. Nobody listens— and then everyone disagrees.")

You don't get the best ones when you are looking for them, but you find them in the course of your normal reading. Obviously, the better read you are, the more material you will have to draw on. History, ancient to modern; economics, classical to contemporary; philosophy—the more you know the better.

A favorite source that meets my own need for wisdom, humor, and irony, consistent with a convincing frame of reference for speakers and for audiences is the "They Said It" department of *Sports Illustrated*.

Art Linkletter was wrong. Children don't say the darnedest things (except for mine). Athletes do. Some are smart, some are dumb. But *Sports Illustrated* catches them at their best, and the writer's craft and ear can be brought to bear here with great effect. The best thing about athletes is that most executive speakers and their audiences have probably heard of them—or they could have heard of them.

And when you use these quotes, you don't create any undue suspicion that the speaker or his staff spent the afternoon at the library. If you want your audience to think of your speakers as experts on the subject at hand, don't prompt the listeners to wonder whether the speaker is spending too much time reading and not enough running the business.

Here are two quotations from *SI* that I have used on more than one occasion, and which have been picked up again and again by other writers.

Dan Quisenberry, retired relief pitcher for the Kansas

City Royals: "I have seen the future, and it's just like the present, only longer."

Jim McMahon, professional quarterback, when asked what it was like to go to Brigham Young University: "They let us chase girls, but they wouldn't let us catch them."

6.5 Manipulating Quotations

Just for fun, try and jot down some situations where you could use these quotations. When you find you're inexorably drawn to such old saws as, "The more things change, the more they remain the same" and, "Those who do not know history are doomed to repeat it," try the Quisenberry line instead.

McMahon's comment is very useful for decrying paternalism or excessive government interference in the affairs of business.

The question remains of how you manipulate a quotation artfully. After all, it has to be there for a reason. It has to come from somewhere and it has to lead somewhere else. And you have to be considerate of your audience. The McMahon quote leaves you open to charges of offending both Mormons and women.

Here's an opening that takes care of all these problems (well, most of them—almost anything you can say will offend *someone*). The sexual and fiscal politics implied are for demonstration purposes and don't necessarily coincide with my own views (or with reality):

There's a story about a hell-raising pro quarterback who attended a sectarian college, noted for its stern morality in this permissive age. Asked what it was like to go to school there, he answered, "They let us chase girls, but they wouldn't let us catch them."

Now, I'm in two minds about this statement. On the one hand, as the father of a teenage girl, I say, "Lock the door and throw away the key."

But as an adult, I feel that we ought to face the facts. Namely, that risk-taking activity is rarely undertaken without some expectation on the part of the risk takers that they will enjoy compensation for their efforts. And if all parties are consenting adults, you ought to let them make the choices for their own reasons, fully mindful of the dangers as well as the possible rewards.

This comes to mind because of the continuing debate over taxation of capital gains. The current treatment of capital gains arrives courtesy of the tax act of 1988, which mandates that capital gains be taxed as current income in the year in which they are realized. The theory, of course, is that this levels the playing field for different kinds of income, removing the tax subsidy for uneconomic investment. But, as Eli Schwartz, professor of economics and finance at Lehigh University, has pointed out, the treatment of capital gains under the current tax code actually punishes investment in the most important sectors of our economy—the corporations that are the basis of our standing in the global economy. He writes, "The corporation pays 34 percent on its return to its equity capital. . . . dividends when paid are taxed at the full personal income-tax rate and any successful reinvestment of retained earnings is again taxed at the full personal rate when realized as capital gains. The overall tax on the return from equity (implicit and explicit) is at least 62 percent, well above the tax on any other source of income."

This punitive taxation of investment income seems to stem from the persistent attitude that investment income is somehow unearned, displaying a serious misunderstanding of the nature of risk-taking activity. You'd think by now that Congress would get the connection between investment, jobs, economic growth, and votes. But no. They still think that people invest just for the fun of the chase. The truth is that while there's no sure payoff at the end of the chase, investors, like football players, are motivated by the possibility of some reward. If all parties are willing, then they ought to be able to enjoy it.

6.6 "Quoting" Without Quotation Marks

Don't feel compelled always to put it in quotation marks. Paraphrase. Change things. Play off them. Have fun. Forgive me for saying this but, as T. S. Eliot more or less put it, "Bad writers are influenced. Good writers steal."

You have to be careful, of course. Senator Joseph Biden was drummed out of the 1988 Democratic presidential campaign for lifting the rhetoric, indeed the life, of Neil Kinnock, head of Britain's Labour Party. Chances are, however, that no one will catch you using proven material, and of course, if it works once, it should work again.

Whether you are quoting or stealing, however, there is

potential for embarrassment. If you're quoting, you have to avoid sounding pretentious on the one hand, and trite on the other.

If you are lifting material, there are dangers other than just being caught plagiarizing. There's such a thing as guilt by association. You don't want to get caught plagiarizing from the wrong people. George Bush made a speech about drugs in which he said that drug users could "almost hear the doors slamming shut." This was lifted directly from a Michael J. Fox TV commercial about drug abuse. And some time later, the president made a pitch for his party on the grounds that the Republicans represented "the heartbeat of America." That was a line from a Chevrolet commercial. I'm not sure that Madison Avenue is the alternative to *Bartlett's* that the world is looking for.

Many people would argue that the demise of classical education has made our rhetoric poorer. My late boss Will Sparks (whom you met earlier) edited some of the Chicago Great Books series. He could speak credibly about being part of the "great conversation," and had worked as a speechwriter in the Johnson White House as well as in corporate America. His work was sprinkled with great quotes and references, but he wrote eloquently in a voice all his own (or not his own—he was a speechwriter, after all).

The Bush story would indicate, perhaps, that modern speechwriters don't read enough and spend too much time watching TV (after all, his writers used these lines, and I recognized the quotes).

CHAPTER
7

Humor—Laughing Matters

Humor is an important element of all but the most somber speeches. But you must consider speakers' natural styles in deciding how funny you want them to be. Some are naturally witty, and can deliver funny lines with the requisite timing. Others can't get a laugh with a can of nitrous oxide. Sometimes the funny ones will want to be absolutely serious, which is easy enough. You've got a harder job if they're stiff and want to be funny. Then, too, standards for humor are pretty high. Anyone who can stay up late enough can watch Jay Leno or David Letterman. Their jokes are fresh and topical, their delivery very professional. And they are poised enough to get laughs even if the jokes don't work.

Some noncomedians have the advantage of audience sympathy to compensate for lack of technique. Landon Parvin, a Washington joke writer, observed in the *New York Times* that "when someone becomes president he is automatically funnier because people are readier to laugh. There's something psychological with the power of the presidency. It makes it easier to get a laugh for the president than if the same joke was used by a senator or a secretary of state."

You have to be careful with humor. It should be appropriate to the audience and to the subject. It can serve to warm up the speaker or the audience, or it can be pointed. But be careful of how sharp the point is. Sarcasm, literally "flesh rending," can backfire, creating sympathy for the opposite point of view. Or, though appropriate for the immediate audience, it may generate bad publicity.

7.1 Ethnic and Sexist Jokes

Victor Kiam, owner of the New England Patriots, compounded the bad publicity stemming from his football team's treatment of a female reporter by telling a sexist joke about her. He later apologized and claimed that he hadn't meant any harm. He only told the joke because he thought it was funny. Lots of people didn't. Ethnic and sexist jokes have a way of blowing up in your face.

Once in a while you can get away with it—if the stereotype flatters the audience, for instance. An audience in Milan didn't mind this one:

> There's a joke going around New York about the possible division of labor in the new Europe. I won't tell the full joke on the grounds of good taste, but suffice it to say that under a scenario code-named Heaven, the Italians

are the lovers and the Swiss are the administrators. Under the alternative scenario, code-named Hell, it's the other way around.

I'm not sure how the Swiss would have taken it.

One speaker I wrote for had to give a talk in Australia and asked me if I knew any Australian jokes. I told him about the Englishman who arrived at Sydney airport only to discover that he had left his passport at home. So he told the immigration officials that he had gone to Oxford with the British ambassador who would surely vouch for him until another passport could be prepared. Sure enough, a phone call provided the needed assurances. The gentleman would merely have to answer a few questions.

But as the questions went on and on, the Englishman grew more and more irritated until at last they asked, "Do you have a criminal record?" To which he replied, "No, I didn't realize you still needed one to get into Australia."

My speaker told this joke as if it had happened to him when he arrived the previous day. And the Aussies, who don't seem at all sensitive about their heritage as a British penal colony, loved it, and were extremely responsive to the speech that followed—which wasn't bad either.

You will note that both these ethnic jokes were extremely gentle. They didn't make anyone out to be stupid, dishonest, or any of the other stereotypes that are at the heart of most ethnic jokes. Stronger than this, I wouldn't get.

Both these jokes depend for their humor on a shared

frame of reference. The Italian audience knows the Swiss reputation for efficiency and their own for amorousness. The Australians know their own national history. When you are writing funny lines for speeches you have to make a judgment about whether people will get the joke.

Landon Parvin puts the problem this way: "What you do is take the truth and skew it a bit. The laugh basically comes in the truth."

7.2   Being Mean

Parvin wrote the following joke for former Democratic Party chairman Robert Strauss:

> Now there's Richard Darman, who we haven't discussed. I had lunch with Dick the other day, and he was complaining about what the Hill thought of him, what the press wrote about him, and so on. Finally, he said, "Bob, why do people take such an instant dislike to me?" I said, "Because it saves time."

What's acceptable at a Gridiron Club roast may not be acceptable everywhere. Parvin says, "It's got to have some slight cut to it, some snap, but the danger at events like the Gridiron is that the punch will come from below the belt, and it's a very fine line. Comedians have the luxury of trying out their material at a comedy club or on the road. You open and close the same night. You never have a chance of trying out your material."

7.3 Foolproof Humor

There is one foolproof method. Pinch well-tested material from people you know are funny. Again, make sure that it is appropriate for your speaker. Mark Twain is good for posterity. For the last generation of executives, Robert Benchley was perfect. For this generation, the essays of Woody Allen and Dave Barry are more appropriate.

CHAPTER
8

Good Stories, Dynamite Facts,
and Other Ways to Enliven Your
Speech

8.1 Using Good Stories to Make a Point

A speechwriter is constantly on the lookout for good stories to liven up his work. If you are more organized than I am, you keep files to stash clippings and notes from your reading. If you're like me, you will just take the chance that you'll remember enough of what you're reading to come through in a pinch. When you learn to think like a speechwriter, you will know the real thing when you see it.

To help you get started, here's a recent piece I ran across in *The Economist*, which is an exceptional source of good stuff because it presents contemporary events in their historical context.

> One of America's earliest takeover battles was in 1868, when Cornelius Vanderbilt fought Jay Gould, Jim Fisk, and Daniel Drew for the Erie Railroad. This trio controlled it, but did not own most of the shares. Their successful defense, apart from moving their headquarters

to a New Jersey hotel protected by a gang and three cannons, was to issue themselves a mountain of new shares (which was illegal, but they bribed the judges). The following year a battle between Erie and another railway, the Albany and Susquehanna, ended in a real fight between two armies of thugs.

The nice thing about a story like this is that it can be used to add weight to almost any point of view. You can use it to attack or defend the spirit of the 1980s, depending on whether you sympathize with raider or raided. There's greed on both sides of this issue: the takeover side is monopolistic and destructive of an enterprise people have worked hard to build. And what about the defenders? It's a long way from bribing judges, cannons, and gangs of goons to greenmail. Or is it? You choose the lesson.

If you really want to be thoughtful, you can even swipe the *Economist*'s thinking:

> The tactics have changed. But there is nothing new about takeovers, as such. What changes . . . is why they happen and how they take place. And this is not determined by the culture or the rapaciousness of financiers. It is set by two main things: the economic circumstances of the day, and the way in which the firms are owned.

8.2 Dynamite Facts

A smaller version of this is what some people call the "factoid," but what I prefer to call "the dynamite fact," a term I once heard Nora Ephron use. Her example, as I recall, was that 75 percent of all swinging couples eat chips with dip before they swing, or before they couple— whatever the term is.

For your purposes, the dynamite fact might be a little less dynamite, or then again it might not, depending on the audience. An example would be the item that in what we used to call the Soviet Union, toilet paper was sold not in grocery stores but in stationery stores, which some foreigners only discovered when they wrote home to ask their friends to send them some. Almost any little slice of Soviet life can serve your purposes.

Dynamite facts are ubiquitous these days. At the low end, look at *USA Today*. It's full of lists of facts and figures, waiting for specious conclusions to be drawn. At the higher end, there's the *Harper's* Index, waiting for the same thing.

Like Tinker Toys or Legos, dynamite facts can be assembled in infinite combinations to make the point you want. Two examples, paired in chapter 11, are that Davidoff, the great Swiss cigar company, gave up buying Havana cigars because the quality had deteriorated, and that Castro himself had given up his trademark smoking habit years before.

Another example is that an English insurance company bought some Italian insurance companies, including a car insurer, in anticipation of the economic unification of Europe in 1992, only to sell them at a loss because it couldn't manage them profitably.

8.3 Colorful New Terms

Keep an eye out for new, colorful terminology, as distinct from business jargon, Pentagonese, legalese, and other language of the priesthood. For example, I like the term "trend surfing," which I recently saw in the *Wall Street Journal*. Trend surfing is faddishness by way of the fad of wind surfing.

8.4 Putting Them Together

How do you put these modules together in a speech? Try this:

We've embarked on the era of global business. But many global ventures are doomed to failure because companies are pursuing it for its own sake, without any real understanding of new markets.

Globality is merely the result of the cumulative business decisions of executives to pursue new marketing opportunities around the world. Yet, many of us have treated it like something we have to do just because everyone else is doing it, like going to the right art galleries or the right parties.

Those who treat globalism as an exercise in "trend surfing" are doomed to failure. For all our declared global outlook, we must still account for differences in laws, habits, and customs. One English insurance company bought several small Italian companies in anticipation of the unification of Europe in 1992, on the assumption that insurance was insurance and it knew insurance. What it didn't know was *Italian* insurance, particularly Italian *auto* insurance. If only one member of senior management had been stuck in a traffic jam in Rome, they might have saved their shareholders millions of pounds.

8.5 Writing for the Eye

Images are as important for speeches as they are for poems. Good ideas can be expressed in visual terms, or supported in visual terms at least as effectively as in cool logical ones. If you can get pictures floating through people's heads rather than news tickers, you're in good shape. Try Martin Luther King's "I have a dream" speech.

I have a dream today that one day the state of Alabama, whose governor's lips are presently dripping with the words of interposition and nullification, will be transformed into a situation where little black boys and black girls will be able to join hands with little white boys and white girls and walk together as sisters and brothers.

I have a dream today that one day every valley shall be exalted, every hill and mountain shall be made low, the rough places will be made plains, and the crooked places will be made straight. . . .

An unbroken stream of pictures, cascading images, all highly moral in tone, and—or so it seemed back in

1961—somehow well within our reach. That's vision, and, set against the backdrop of the Washington Monument, delivered in that rolling, ministerial voice, it's oratory at its most powerful in my lifetime. Contemporary speakers are generally lacking on every score, especially the vision thing.

Business speeches have real possibilities in this line. After all, businesses provide for human needs. Agribusiness feeds far more people than subsistence farming. Pharmaceutical companies cure the sick. Chemical companies protect the food supply.

In general, companies that make "stuff" have more visual possibilities than service businesses. They conjure up images of workers, machinery, useful items rolling off assembly lines. Or, depending on how you look at it, they also suggest dark satanic mills, unemployment lines, and specters haunting Europe.

Try this:

Responsible companies have been exploring other options for waste disposal. For example, in areas where geological conditions are right, toxic wastes can be safely injected into deep underground wells, natural cavities or abandoned mineshafts thousands of feet below the earth's surface and well below any usable ground water. . . . Organic or petroleum wastes can be fed to special strains of bacteria—superbugs—that break down chemicals into harmless substances. . . . You and I and the nine-times-our-weight in trash we produce every year are also responsible. Remember, that can of insect repellent, the leftover prescription drug, the chlorine from your swimming pool, your hair spray, that synthetic-fabric shirt, the broken plastic toy, that half-used can of paint, the old car polish, and household cleaner—your trash— is heading for the town dump where it could combine with other chemically produced goods of modern living, and, under the wrong circumstances, create a hazardous situation.

These days, the service sector dominates the economy. More people work in service industries than in manufacturing or agriculture, so chances are you have an "image problem." Health care is an easy one because it's about saving lives, but law is a bit harder, and fast-food restaurants are harder still.

I spend most of my time writing about financial subjects. The English call finance and related fields "invisibles," and with good reason. The pictorial possibilities are more limited than those of automobiles or amber waves of grain.

Currency is the favored medium of several popular artists these days, as well as drug traffickers. Finance these days is more about making electronic bookkeeping entries, not the things money will buy, like houses and food. Or what it can create, like factories and jobs. Much of modern finance is really ideas about money or even ideas about ideas about money. Look at the jargon— derivative instruments, S&P futures, REMICs, repos, interest-rate swaps. Finance is at several removes from "stuff" as we know it.

Look at the trouble Sherman McCoy had explaining his

work as a bond trader to his daughter in Tom Wolfe's novel *Bonfire of the Vanities*:

"A bond is a way of loaning people money. Let's say you want to build a road, and it's not a little road but a big highway, like the highway we took up to Maine last summer. Or you want to build a big hospital. Well, that requires a lot of money, more money than you could ever get by just going to a bank. So what you do is, you issue what are called bonds."

"You build roads and hospitals, Daddy? That's what you do?"

Tough, isn't it? But McCoy's wife finds the right common denominator. "Just imagine that a bond is a slice of cake, and you didn't bake the cake, but every time you hand somebody a slice of the cake a tiny little bit comes off, like a little crumb, and you can keep that."

To find imagery for subjects as abstract as these, look for the social utility of what you're talking about. Trace the financial instrument back up the food chain to the place where it intersects with people's lives. For high interest on credit cards, that point is the fact that higher rates allow you to cast a wider net for customers, extending credit to people who really need it, and can afford it, but wouldn't have access to it if all bankers were like Scrooge. Tighter credit standards reserve credit for the rich and drive people with less money into the arms of loan sharks.

You can see this social utility in most of the service

industries. Fast-food restaurants bring work to urban areas where manufacturing jobs are scarce, for example. I have a tough time with the 900 telephone-number business, but pay me enough money and I'll find social utility in almost anything except cigarette smoking.

And if it's for a good cause, I'll do it for nothing. I once had to do a quick speech for a friend who purchased my services in a fund-raising auction for our local nursery school. I figured I'd get a wedding speech or a toast. No such luck. This fellow had to address a convention of computer-satellite time buyers. He was on a panel with three people who were selling products, and his own product wasn't ready yet. He talked to me about his business for two hours and I didn't understand a word he said, so I asked him to tell me some war stories. Pay dirt. In listening to him talk, I settled on how computer technology can really make the economy more efficient. One story we used was from his days as a computer consultant. He advised a data-processing manager for a trucking firm to buy a few PCs and some new software to replace his mainframes, which would save hundreds of thousands of dollars a year:

> The fellow told me, "You don't understand what this is all about. It's not about saving money. It's not about efficiency." He took me to a window that looked out on a refrigerated room, full of mainframes and technicians in sanitary uniforms, and he said, "This is what it's about." He went on, "I'm sure you're correct about the savings. I'm sure that the PCs and the software are so easy that

anyone can use them. But if anyone can use them, they don't need these, and if they don't need these, they don't need me."

8.6 Negative Constructions

"Lots of people should be grateful to these soldiers and sailors for all they did."

Doesn't sound so good, does it? Try this instead.

"Never in the field of human conflict was so much owed by so many to so few." Thus Winston Churchill.

Obviously, negative constructions can be powerful, but in general, try to stick to positive language. The word *not,* as Strunk and White point out, is particularly weak, often used as a means of evasion. It makes for unconvincing rhetoric. But sometimes it's hard to avoid. You may be working to a tight deadline and struggling to make a strong case for an idea you don't believe in. For example, you may feel more comfortable saying, "It's not inconceivable that if we end the tax on capital gains, we will abolish poverty in our lifetime," instead of "When we end the capital gains tax we will certainly abolish poverty in our lifetime." The first is a more modest claim. Conceivable, yes. Certain or even probable, no.

Try making a positive case for the health effects of smoking. You're stuck with things like, "No one has ever caught a tar molecule provoking a lung cell to metastasize into a malignancy." No wonder it's easier to say, "Sin taxes fall most heavily on those who can least afford them."

Negative construction can help you lower the common denominator, but while what you are writing may not be untrue, strictly speaking, people won't believe it either. When a speaker implies what he is by saying what he is not, or suggests what he believes by saying that he does not believe in its opposite, the audience doesn't believe him. He doth protest too much. Audiences believe plain speakers, and plain speakers say what they mean, they don't disagree with what they don't mean. Now, do I mean what I said, or do I not mean what I didn't say?

Another problem—purely mechanical, but very important to the speechwriter nevertheless—is the chance of misunderstanding. The speaker may drop the negation, or swallow it, or someone may cough, and suddenly, the audience may have the idea that the speaker is saying the opposite of what he means.

You can see the headlines now. "Prez confesses, 'I am (cough) a crook.' "

CHAPTER
9

Being Forceful

9.1 Modesty

That's not to say that you can't score a few points by acknowledging that your own position wasn't necessarily handed to you on top of Mount Sinai, or can't reasonably be challenged by those who think otherwise. Wait, let me try that again.

You can win a few points by admitting that you may be fallible. You don't want your speaker to look arrogant up there. Self-assured, yes. Content in the wisdom of his positions, yes, but open-minded enough to entertain the possibility that others are contributing to the discussion in good faith.

Qualify statements with words such as "likelihood" and "often" rather than "certainty" or "always."

9.2 If You're Going to Be Arrogant, at Least Be Clever

Sometimes, of course, yours is the only logical position and you can't resist stating it in definitive terms.

As an example, I'd like to return to the issue of whether banks should be able to branch across state lines, which I mentioned earlier in another context. This was a very emotional issue during the 1980s (and remains so, although things have changed legally a great deal). The regional bankers' plan to allow branching across state lines only in contiguous states—as long as those contiguous states didn't include New York, California, or Illinois—was clearly protectionist, but presented as a move in the direction of greater competitiveness. I wanted my speaker to attack the regional idea and discredit it without necessarily calling the opposing speakers a bunch of hypocrites out to feather their own nests.

I had him tell the story of the Miami pizza wars, during which eleven new pizzerias were bombed by "entrenched pizza interests." "The method may be different," I wrote, "but the principle is the same." It certainly put those preaching the opposing point of view on the defensive.

9.3 Emphasis

If you're working hard, say you're working hard. Don't say you're working "intensely." If you have finished a project ahead of schedule, say you've beaten your deadline, don't say it's a "rapid achievement."

You don't add to anyone's appreciation of your performance by sounding as though you are proud of it. Let the recitation of ideas and facts convince them of your authority. Adjectives, adverbs, and modifying phrases can't do it. Give them benchmarks.

"I hit fifty-four home runs in 1920, an extraordinary achievement." This means nothing to an audience that knows nothing about baseball. After all, basketball players score thousands of points a year. Say instead, "I hit twenty-nine homers in 1919, a new record, and then broke it the following year with fifty-four. Before that, only one other batter had ever hit as many as twenty-one."

9.4 Repetition for Emphasis and Meaning

When you are writing for the ear, not the eye, the listener needs to have his thinking organized for him. That's what you are doing. Good ideas shouldn't just be dealt with in passing. They should be repeated, with some variation, for best effect.

Good things come in threes. A series of three related or parallel facts, phrases, ideas, or variations will reinforce the point, as well as lend special significance to the ideas. And it sounds terrific.

The best single example I can think of is "of the people, by the people, and for the people."

9.5   Playing the Numbers—Using Statistics

Audiences won't remember masses of information and statistics, so don't shovel it at them unless in support of some point that they will remember. Or if the point is weak, you may use them to deliberately fudge the issue— remember Mark Twain's adage about "lies, damned lies, and statistics." We all get caught with a weak case once in a while.

Mickey Kaus, who wrote for Senator Ernest Hollings in 1988, has pointed out the sometimes tenuous relationship between facts and the truth in political speechwriting. "In presidential campaigns, the 'message' comes first. Then speechwriters insert the facts to back it up, preferably startling facts. This process does not lend itself to startling accuracy. Ronald Reagan set the standard here, which is lax."

Facts cut to fit the message are a staple across the political spectrum. Kaus went on to choose some numbers that he expected would crop up in the '92 race, along with the real facts behind them. For example:

". . . and it's a disgrace that three million Americans are homeless each night." The three million number was promoted by homeless advocates in the mid-'80s. Not even they bother to defend it anymore. What's the right number? Clearly higher than the 250,000 homeless the census actually counted one day last year. A 1988 study by Martha Burt of the Urban Institute came up with

600,000 as a maximum estimate. Any number between 250,000 and 600,000 is defensible, and still a disgrace.

Here's another:

"Between now and the year 2000, most new entrants into the work force will be minorities." A "net" vs. "gross" scam is at work here. As Lawrence Mishel and Ruy Teixeira note in a recent paper, white non-Hispanics will still make up the vast majority (66.8 percent) of people entering the work force. But because they will also be the vast majority of people *leaving* the work force, their contribution of "net"—or "new"—workers will be less than 50 percent. The work force will become a bit less white. But its majority won't be minority anytime soon, if ever.

You get the picture. Don't believe everything you hear in speeches any more than you believe anything you read in the papers. On the other hand, if you do hear a "fact" somewhere, that's usually good enough reason to use it again, if it suits your argument. Ultimately, your speaker is accountable for the veracity of his material, so if your speaker is highly contentious or your subject controversial, try a bit harder.

9.6 Getting More Out of Statistics

Having said that, here are a few tips. Use dramatic statistics. "The new-issue market for junk bonds has grown geometrically over the last decade, from $1.5

billion in 1978 to $7.4 billion in 1983, to $48 billion in 1986." Notice how well this works. The increase from '78 to '83 was also geometric, but it was only $5.9 billion. Peanuts.

When you are using statistics, you should interpret them for the audience. For example, if you say, "Our cost of borrowing went from 8.5 percent to 10 percent in a period of only six months," the uninitiated might think, "well, that's only one-and-a-half percent."

You might elaborate, "Our cost of borrowing went from 8.5 percent to 10 percent in only six months. That's a lot. Capital is a raw material. It's no less a raw material for us than steel or oil. Its cost rose by 188 percent in only six months, and it's still rising. If oil and steel were going up by 18 percent in six months, people would be talking about our country becoming another Brazil."

Or how about: "When you ponder that the value of merger and acquisition transactions was $167.5 billion last year, or about 23 percent of gross private domestic investment, you can understand why we're having trouble competing in world markets. These investments produce no new wealth. Rather they fit Robert Sarnoff's definition of finance: the passing of money from hand to hand until it disappears."

9.7   Using Statistics to Tell Stories

Sometimes, however, statistics can be more than a tool for advancing an argument. Numbers can tell stories if they're the right numbers and if they're in the hands of an inspired storyteller. The following speech by a chemical industry executive to an audience of farm-credit bankers represents an excellent example:

What is your life worth? I suppose that is a shocking question to some of you. And I imagine it is a question that others of you have never thought about. Yet it is a question you ask yourself daily—and answer in all sorts of ways.

For example, if you travel by commercial plane, you take a three-in-a-million risk. But if you drive, your risk is closer to two hundred in a million. Those of you who farm actively might be interested in knowing that your career choice puts you roughly in the same occupational risk category as an airline pilot—six hundred in a million. But if you regularly drive a tractor, you add to that risk.

Suppose you are a heavy smoker; your chances for a long life diminish seriously—to a three-in-a thousand risk. But if your vice is a daily bottle of beer, there are fewer than three chances out of one hundred thousand you'll regret it. Make that beer a dry martini, and you increase those regrets, often rather quickly.

Of course, someone is bound to ask about the statistics for a combination of these risks. Well, if you happen to be a heavy-smoking, beer-drinking tractor driver who came to this meeting by car, and had two martinis for lunch . . . the odds are that you're not going to be around to hear the end of my speech.

I think you've all got the idea. Everything we do in life involves some element of risk.

Of course, our government could legislate away some of these risks. For example, when the speed limit was reduced to 55 miles per hour during the energy crisis, we discovered that it saves lives. By limiting speed still further, more lives could be saved. And by reducing the speed limit to 10 miles per hour we could virtually eliminate traffic deaths.

On the other hand, at ten miles per hour, it would have taken some of you four days to travel from Springfield to Rochester (that's about the speed of a covered wagon) and the sheer frustration of that slow drive would have accounted for significant rises in blood pressure.

Even if ten-mile-per-hour speeds would eliminate our 50,000 yearly traffic deaths, it's not a very effective tradeoff. To save those lives, we would cripple our transportation system and bring much of the economy to a standstill—which wouldn't improve anybody's health. Besides, the public wouldn't stand for it.

I admit this is an extreme example. But it doesn't take genius to discern that the benefits of some life-saving regulations come nowhere near the staggering cost to society of their implementation.

The benefit of permitting a reasonable national speed limit far exceeds any risk you drivers take. That's a risk/benefit judgment and you make it.

And so on. The statistics here are an integral part of the speech. The speaker is in the business of convincing people that regulatory zeal, in trying to reduce the risk from use of chemicals in farming, constitutes a far greater threat to society than the purely arithmetic occurrence of chemically induced disease. He goes on to say:

New technology has created anxieties that did not exist before. For example, some scientists have analyzed the aflatoxin occurring naturally in peanuts. They've calculated that eating four tablespoons of peanut butter a day produces liver-cancer risks of four in one hundred thousand. Whether or not you agree with the megadoses they fed animals to arrive at that figure, you may notice that it is about the same low-level risk as drinking diet soda containing saccharin. Funny, isn't it, that nobody in Washington has proposed banning peanut butter.

And now I'm going to end this section abruptly. After all, as Ernest Hemingway (Nobel Prize, 1954) said (or was it Sparky Lyle, Cy Young Award, 1977?), the end is the hardest part to write.

Section 4

PARTS OF A
SPEECH

Every speech should have a beginning, a middle, and
an end. A friend of mine who used to work for the State
Department and the CIA described the three parts like
this. "Tell 'em what you're gonna' tell 'em; tell 'em; and
tell 'em what you just told 'em."

That's pretty elemental, and certainly true for speeches
in which the purpose isn't so much to persuade as to
inform, take it or leave it. In speeches like that, the voice
is the government, not the individual. There's an approved point of view, an approved version of the truth.
But in corporate life, the approach should be tempered a
bit. The point of view may be collective, but the voice
should be personal.

CHAPTER
_10_

Beginnings

A good opening is important. If you lose the audience at the outset, you're going to have a tough time hooking them again later on. You want the audience to buy your speaker as a person, to buy the logic and information of the speech, and, ultimately, the company's version of things, and it all begins at the beginning.

There are several threads. You must introduce the subject—tell 'em what you're gonna tell 'em—and you must also establish your speaker with the audience, and settle his own butterflies.

10.1 Ahem—Getting Started

The beginning really consists of two parts—throat clearing and the joke, which I discussed briefly in chapter 4, in talking about how to apportion time in a speech. A minute of throat clearing and two minutes of joke. Throat clearing is the informal words that a speaker uses to accustom himself to being in front of his audience and to orient himself to the occasion. It's not easy to write the throat clearing because when you're writing, you can't anticipate what may happen when it comes time to give the speech.

I once had to write a speech for delivery in Europe on the day after a presidential election, and of course the speaker had to leave the weekend before it. I gave him two leads, to encompass any outcome. I had the same problem with a Super Bowl one year: the whole speech was structured around football, but again, the appropriate lead was subject to the outcome of the game.

Less topical throat clearing might include some reference to the weather, the location, or the time of day, which you can sometimes anticipate. You may also prime your speaker to respond to "that generous introduction" or to the remarks of previous speakers.

Consider the time of day. If it's breakfast and the audience has been traveling the night before (or partying), you might get things rolling with some remark about the medicinal and restorative qualities of strong coffee.

If the crowd is likely to be smoking after-dinner cigars and drinking brandy, or planning to go out to play golf after the session, you can be rather expansive. My friend Richard Sorenson, having noted that his speaker was scheduled for two hours at a conference in sunny Puerto Rico, put a line in the introduction saying that the organizers must somehow have gotten the speaker mixed up with Fidel Castro. Be careful with lines like this, however. In this case, people have to be familiar with the fact that Castro is famous for being able to go on for hours at a time; not everyone knows that.

10.2 Hit 'Em Where They Live

One way of winning an audience over with some throat-clearing material is to say nice, thoughtful things about the audience and the surroundings. Here's an example that's perfectly attuned to its audience, from A. W. Clausen, chairman of Bank of America:

> I'm delighted to be here in Vancouver and honored to be your guest at the first Executive Day program to be held in western Canada. I know it gets cold in Canada, but wherever you find a single Canadian, you find the warmth of humanity. This is a country where manners still count for something . . . where neighbors still help neighbors . . . where cities not only deliver efficient services, but are clean and livable. And that's as good a definition of civilization as I can muster.

What Canadian wouldn't (pardon the expression) warm to Clausen after that? You can't ask for a more sympathetic opening. It demonstrates a knowledge of and appreciation for Canadian character and quality of life, and, coming from a U.S. speaker, it implies a sense of the loss of these qualities south of the border without actually stating it. That might not play back in San Francisco, but Canadians like to hear it.

10.3   Launching the Argument

The *second* part of the beginning sets the stage for your argument. It may be a joke, an anecdote, a quotation, or a new item. Whatever it is, it should be interesting in its own right.

10.4   Choosing the Right Opening

Many factors should be weighed in choosing the type of opening you want. The subject may be too grave to lend itself to a funny treatment. Flatter your audience by assuming that they are knowledgeable and witty people, but don't overestimate their sophistication. On the other hand, you may want to be serious, and if so, you have to decide whether you want to sound somber, wise, or merely reflective.

10.5   The Right Opening Is Hard to Write

The correct beginning is usually the hardest part of a speech to write. Father Peter Carey spends about half his sermon-writing time on the opening. That's a lot, but of course he has to answer to a higher authority than most of us. I wouldn't say that I spend half my time on the opening, at least not half my time at the word processor, although when I have a tough assignment it may keep me up the night before I start.

Regardless of the time, the beginning takes some of the most serious effort. Not only do you have to put your speaker at ease and win over the audience, you're also setting the tone for the rest of the speech. The opening will dictate the tenor and logic of what's to come. A quotation, anecdote, or joke can point to or even summarize the larger message of the speech. Find the correct opening and sometimes the rest of the speech writes itself.

CHAPTER
11

Different Types of Openings

11.1   Videotape

If you have the resources, the joke doesn't even have to be written or delivered by the speaker. While I normally hate relying on visual aids, a well-chosen videotape can be the best introduction of all, such as the use of a *60 Minutes* segment on the controversial pesticide Alar, which brought the "enemy" right into the auditorium. To introduce a speech on the special pitfalls of bank PR, I used a scene from W. C. Fields's movie *The Bank Dick* in which Fields, playing a bank security guard, struggles to subdue a little boy in a cowboy suit playing with a gun. Use gimmicks like this if you can.

11.2   News Items and Dynamite Facts

Keep a sharp eye out for offbeat news items and dynamite facts. I've gotten substantial mileage out of the fact, mentioned in chapter 8, that Davidoff, the great Swiss cigar merchant, stopped selling Havana cigars a few years ago.

How can you use such an item? Try this:

As absolute ruler of Cuba, Castro is, in effect, CEO of all Cuban enterprises. But he forgot, or never learned, that you have to please your customers. Castro himself had very prominently stopped smoking a few years before, and so he lost touch with what his customers valued in a smoke. If he had kept on smoking, he might have realized that quality was slipping. He might have understood that the brand name is more important than where the product is made. "Davidoff" is what implies quality to Davidoff customers, not "Havana."

Yet you don't have to be a Communist dictator to forget this elementary rule of the marketplace. As our comrades in Detroit have learned painfully over the past twenty-five years, there may not be any magic in the name Ford, GM, or Chrysler either.

11.3   Headlines

A staple technique is to orient the speech in terms of the day's news, or historical context. I used to write for a man who was at the time instrumental in averting what appeared to be an imminent and inevitable international economic collapse. A recitation of doom-and-gloom headlines provided an engaging and funny introduction for a speech in which the principal message was an inherent lack of drama. "Terror that the world would end with a bang gave way to the fear that it would end with a whimper. And now that this hasn't happened either some of us have begun to suspect that it might not end at all." His public image was of a man who could keep his head while all around him were losing theirs. We kept the rhetoric calm, and let others supply the hysterics.

11.4   Humor to Open

While I discussed humor generically in chapter 6, I'd like to talk more about it here as it specifically applies to opening a speech. This is not throwaway humor. It's used to relax the speaker, disarm the audience, and plunge them into the heart of the discussion as painlessly as possible. The ground rules for using humor described earlier still apply—nonethnic, nonracist, fairly kind, and so forth. But humor can be instructive, and you should look for the instructive potential in it.

11.5   Cartoons

Cartoons in the *New Yorker* magazine are another good source of openings, particularly for rush jobs, because just about every issue will reflect some hot concern of the moment. It may be the very thing you're working on. Just a quick look at the issue of April 29, 1991, my deadline (missed) for turning in the first draft of this book, yields the following:

An elderly woman armed with a pistol is waving the bank manager out of the way so she can get a clear shot at the computer workstation behind him.

"Stand aside, Gruenwald! It's the computer I'm blowing away!" (Useful for a speech on the importance of technology and/or service quality in today's economy.)

A group of people are sitting around a boardroom table—well-integrated by gender, race, and one winged pixie.

The chairman says, "It gives me great pleasure to welcome Jengi, the first sprite to serve on the board of the National Forestry Association." (Useful for talking about the difficulty of satisfying all sensitivities in affirmative action issues.)

A lonely ship is sailing on a vast ocean, with the caption "The Private Doubts of Christopher Columbus." A thought balloon emanating from the ship reads, "It sure looks flat." (Useful for a speech on maintaining one's faith in the idea of free trade in the face of stiff competition from foreign companies.)

Two men in business suits are up to their shoulders in the ocean. One says to the other, "There's no need for alarm—the staff *will* be reduced, but only by attrition." (Useful for talking about the desperate need to cut costs in some companies and the lack of will to do so.)

The nice thing about these cartoons is that they can be quickly and vividly described, they usually get a laugh, and they are instantly profound. Get out the latest *New Yorker* and practice.

11.6   Joke into Message

A joke can get a laugh and establish the tone and theme for the whole speech. Here's one.

> A fellow is driving along a farm road and sees a magnificent pig. He stops to take a closer look. It is indeed a tremendous specimen, but he notices that it is missing one of its hind quarters.
>
> The farmer comes out, and the stranger praises the animal. The farmer says, "Let me tell you about that pig. Two years ago, my family and I were sound asleep when a fire started in the house. The pig smelled the smoke, rooted his way under the bottom of the fence, barreled through the front door of the house, came upstairs, and woke me up. He saved my whole family. Then, last year, I was plowing the south forty when the tractor hit a ditch, toppled over on me, and pinned me. He heard me shouting for help, went under the fence, ran over the fields, and pushed the tractor hard enough to let me escape just before it killed me. Yes, that pig is just like a member of the family."
>
> The stranger was visibly moved. "Gee," he said, "that's some pig, all right. Tell me. How did he lose his leg?"
>
> The farmer smiled and answered, "A pig that good— you don't want to butcher the whole thing at once."

In times like these, American corporations are searching their souls and restructuring on a massive scale. No one is sacred or safe. Well-run organizations that have reinvented themselves regularly over long periods of time, trained and retrained their workers, kept themselves in fighting trim, have found that their financial and marketing postures are untenable in the face of global competition. But the question remains, how should they do it? Sell assets? Take on additional debt to buy back stock? Close plants? Skimp on research and development? As I look around at the results that such exercises have wrought, I can't help but think about that farmer and that pig. "A pig that good—you don't want to butcher the whole thing at once."

CHAPTER
12

The Rest of the Speech

12.1   Keep the Ball Rolling

If the beginning is really good and evocative, you should refer to it throughout the speech. The pig butchered in pieces is very strong, if uncomfortable for some listeners. But it is a useful, emotive metaphor for the serious subject of restructuring corporations in the current difficult economic climate. It suggests an awareness of the pain this process can inflict, but acknowledges the possible consequences if it isn't done in a thoughtful and timely fashion. You can refer to such elements repeatedly.

12.2   Facts That Speak for Themselves

Sometimes the facts are so dynamite that they speak for themselves, and if you've got a chance to use them, do it. Jan Van Meter, who is a terrific speechwriter (and gave me my first two professional assignments) was the one who used the *60 Minutes* segment on Alar to start a speech to the National Pasta Association on the dangers that can befall an industry association when hit with a PR crisis.

He followed up immediately with a litany of events, starting with the announcement of the formation of a new public interest group—Mothers and Others for Pesticide Limits, chaired by Meryl Streep, who was well qualified by virtue of the fact that she's a mother.

In the week after *60 Minutes*, the following mixed messages were heard by the public:

1. Ohio announced that it would test baby food and juices for Alar independently of the federal government.
2. The association for apple growers attacked *60 Minutes*, but announced that Alar was in use on only 5 percent of the United States' apple crop.
3. The EPA said that the NRDC study was misleading, but asked Congress for authority to act faster in removing dangerous pesticides from the market.
4. Associated Press ran a story on consumer panic in Canada, even though Canadian health officials saw no threat to the public.
5. Ohio's governor asked state and federal officials to ban Alar.
6. West Virginia's Agriculture Commissioner helpfully announced to the public that West Virginia's apples were Alar-free.

101

In the second week after *60 Minutes* these things happened:

1. Led by the New York City school system, city after city banned all apples and apple products from their lunchrooms.
2. Some of the apple processors wondered among themselves if they should join with the activists since they clearly couldn't win.
3. The processor association publicly reaffirmed the industry's commitment to the safe use of pesticides (as opposed to what?).
4. Several apple-product companies publicly reaffirmed their ban on Alar and their commitment to consumer health.
5. A scare over Chilean grapes that were supposed to have been poisoned hit the public.

National magazines got on the bandwagon. People worried. Supermarkets announced that their apples were Alar-free. And Meryl Streep was chosen one of the Outstanding Mothers of 1989. Finally, a spokesperson for the Natural Resources Defense Council apologized for the economic damage inflicted on apple growers. Never mind.

Having set up the audience in this way, Jan launched into a series of lessons, which he's very good at since he taught college English before going into PR.

102

1. Be prepared is more than just the Boy Scout's motto.
2. Beware of your friends, especially if they work for the government.
3. Beware of your enemies, period.
4. Being a day late means you'd better catch up.
5. Remember, you're fighting history as well as the crisis of the moment.

And then there was another series of lessons about how to prepare for such a crisis before it happened.

The point about all this documentary rhetoric, from *60 Minutes* through the object lessons, is that it is not fancy, but it is very effective.

12.3   Sustaining the Theme

Here's an example of how a good opening can characterize a whole speech, on the role of science in feeding the hungry people of the world:

> I know a boy who wants to go to the moon. When I was his age—growing up on a farm in the midwest—I wanted to fly in an airplane. My father, at age thirteen, rode in an automobile for the first time.
>
> As a boy, my grandfather wanted to visit Chicago. We've come a long way in a short time—and the world has changed radically.
>
> Yet in this same world there are people who know

nothing about the moonwalk, who will never ride in an airplane, or even a car. Seeing the city is the least of their worries; they haven't enough to eat.

This terse, evocative opening compresses a huge amount of personal, social, and economic history, and uses it to launch a discussion of a topic of enormous importance to us all.

The transition is made gracefully, but powerfully.

I get angry when I hear people talk about the good old days—they were good only to a lucky few. Never in history was there enough food for everyone. Writings of antiquity describe major famines including one that lasted seven years in Egypt. The great hunger in medieval China caused widespread cannibalism. When the potato crop failed in 1846, Ireland lost a quarter of its population. Grain sent from America took months to arrive and no one knew how to process it. The Indian famine of 1877 cost four million lives. During this same period, thirteen million Chinese starved in the worst famine in recorded history. As late as 1921, Russia lost five million to drought in the Ukraine. The good old days—were terrible.

Today, for the first time, the world has the ability to deal with the problems of food production and rapid population growth. Whether, and how, these capabilities will be used is another matter.

If the beginning is your headline, the middle is your story. This is where you cram the ideas that compose your larger thesis, supported by convenient facts and statistics.

It's the stuff that becomes part of the literature on your subject. It will probably take up the bulk of your research time but, ultimately, it is often the easiest part to write. Your time is limited. Use your best arguments. Leave out the weaker ones. You don't have to write with scholarly attention to all sides of the issue (although it strengthens any argument to give the opposing view and then deftly blow it to smithereens). A good speech is persuasive. It doesn't have to be proved with mathematical certainty. It leads audiences to accept your version of an issue.

In the case of the agriculture speech, the body is built around three lessons the chemical industry has learned about dealing with agriculture.

First, concentrate research and development on specific identified problems.

Second, develop the simplest possible technology and adapt it to local conditions so that it will work where it's needed.

Third, move quickly to disperse new technology around the world, so that everyone can benefit from volume production.

Point by point, the industry's record is recounted, including its cooperation with governments and multilateral aid and relief organizations to help solve very large problems. The limitations of private companies in this process are described forthrightly, their real accomplishments stated modestly. Hats off to speaker and writer; the modest farm boy—visionary sensibility delineated in the beginning permeates the entire speech. And this serves very well when it comes to making the most sensitive argument, which is that these companies—despite the fact that they do a lot of good by making agriculture more productive and stopping the spread of disease—are businesses and must be run like businesses to go on doing good. They are not just private research-and-development labs whose products must be turned over free of charge to any and all countries.

Industry research is geared to develop the products *now* that will be needed in the *future* to feed an expanding world.

In order to continue to do this, industry needs to make a reasonable return on its products for long-term investment in research and production capacity. We also need recognition and protection of such intellectual property as patents, trademarks, and licenses. In many countries where multinational companies operate, these rights are being questioned. Some developing nations would like to deny them altogether. It is easy for industry to make a case for the protection of specialized and expensive technology such as computer hardware and weapons, or what many regard as frivolous products such as Coca-Cola. Developing nations need to build food reserves, not armies or soft-drink companies.

But because this need is for food, it sounds hardhearted to argue for the same protection of agricultural patents. Yet products that increase agricultural yields or protect plant and animal growth are developed and made available through much the same process as computer systems and soft drinks. They need the same encouragement and the same protection. It takes eight to ten years and twenty-five million dollars to bring a new agricultural chemical through development into the marketplace. But nothing happens to this new product—this new technology—until someone invests money to build a plant to supply it to a less developed nation or spends marketing money to introduce the product and teach farmers to use it effectively and safely.

And so on.

Take note. The voice of the speaker, who has been a farmer all his life, makes for a much more effective spokesman for the relationship of market economics and agriculture than some economist or business-school grad could ever be.

12.4 The End

Most of what people remember about a speech is said at the end, so make sure it counts. Use it to summarize the points you want people to remember. This is your best opportunity to show how good a writer you are.

The end of the agriculture speech echoes the beginning:

When my grandfather was a boy there were a billion and a half people on earth. He witnessed the advent of synthetic fertilizers and farm machinery to replace the horse and plow.

My father drove a tractor, ran a combine, and planted hybrid corn. There were two billion people.

A man landed on the moon and the world's population

107

doubled in my lifetime. The farmers of my generation used pesticides, herbicides, and the high-yield varieties of the green revolution.

My children take space probes for granted. They could live to see five billion people on earth. They may dine on synthetic foods or enjoy new and better varieties of plants and animals.

And that boy who wants to go to outer space may someday get there. He may set up a thriving experimental farm in a space lab with controlled soil, moisture, and temperature. A farm free of earth's traditional pests and agricultural problems. He may even live in a world where age-old problems are solved by the science and technology that we are developing today.

12.5   Making It Flow

A few words about keeping the flow going. As you move from one point to another, or from the beginning to the middle to the end, it helps to give your listeners some help. Leaps of logic and information that may seem self-evident to readers may not come across to listeners. You may want to lead them from one point to another. You may want to form their conclusions for them.

Constructions that utilize phrases like "on the one hand . . . and on the other"; "first the good news . . . now the bad news"; "in the past . . . now, however," and others can accurately signal that the discussion of a point is continuing. Ask questions raised by the material and then answer them. Don't assume that audiences will necessarily get the connection between facts, stories, and arguments.

Section 5

GIVING AWARDS, ACCEPTING THEM, AND OTHER LIGHTER SPEECH FARE

People can't live on bread alone, and executives can't get by on a steady diet of eight-course rhetoric. Executives don't just run businesses. They have many other roles that they must play. They lend their time, and give their companies' money to many good causes, they must rally their own employees, and so on. Their speeches will reflect these multiple demands on their time. I like to compare the range of speeches I write to items from the major food groups. They are, in order of importance for the speechwriter:

1. Meaty, high-minded fare, rich in protein if the writer is good at his job, and in fat if he isn't; on major topics of the day, of interest to all people who consider themselves good citizens, not just business people.

2. Complex carbohydrates, such as whole-grain breads—industry issues, crucial for understanding by competitors and colleagues alike, as well as the business press.

3. Legumes; taken together, they provide high-quality protein and important trace minerals. These deal with business issues for audiences that are subsets of the industry you are writing about.

4. High protein snacks for energy—company issues, for one's own colleagues as well as investor groups and analysts.

5. Green leafy vegetables—the charitable issues, causes that the executive supports, along with his counterparts from other companies (such as United Way, the IBM of charities).
6. Fruit—company exhortations to participate in such causes as blood drives and political action committees.
7. Desserts—presenting awards, accepting them, and introducing other speakers, both inside the company and out.

In this section I'm going to concentrate on food groups five, six, and seven. Speeches like this are often dull, and there's no good reason for it. There's no such thing as a throwaway speech. Each occasion represents an opportunity for the speaker to score points with an audience, and those points represent money for good causes and good will with other companies, other industries, and with their friends. Things like this will often have more immediate effect on the speaker's life than business results will. So the problem for you as a speechwriter is very important indeed, and you must be diligent and professional. You still want to show the speaker off to good effect. The people who put these events together take them very seriously. They don't want to feel as if they're just ink blots on the speakers' calendars.

111

At the same time, don't be too holy about it. As you will see from the examples, I think you ought to seek the unexpected. Challenge the audience. Make them think and, if possible, have some fun.

CHAPTER
13

Give It a Novel Twist

As the speechwriter, you don't exactly have to spend a lifetime in the library to give one of these occasions, no matter how minor it may seem, your special touch. All it takes is analysis of the occasion, the audience, the subject, a look at the briefing papers supplied by the organizers, and maybe some casual browsing through common reference books. Then, of course, you bring it all together with talent and wit, both of which you possess in abundance.

13.1 Getting to the Pint—The Company Blood Drive

Let's take a speech common to many large companies, the blood drive. Blood banks like to appeal to big companies for participation in their drives because it's a good opportunity to gather substantial quantities of safe blood at a single location. Now we all know how important blood is for the delivery of high-quality health care. Blood is a serious subject, and most speeches about it are pretty serious, too, so serious that you'd rather give an extra pint than listen to them. If you give a dull-but-pious speech on blood, you probably won't disappoint anyone, but no one will remember it either. They'll just dutifully open a vein and go home.

In fact, however, blood and blood transfusion have a fascinating history, and for a friend of mine, a cursory look through the literature once turned up enough lore for a good speech.

I'm delighted to see so many of you here this evening. As business leaders and corporate volunteers in the Greater Metropolitan Blood program, you're probably under the impression that we're here to wind up a successful 1980 donor campaign. That's only partly true. We're also celebrating an important anniversary. It's the 380th birthday of the Reverend Felix Potter, an Anglican clergyman, who would have very much enjoyed being here tonight. In addition to being a churchman, the Reverend Mr. Potter was also a scientific dabbler. In 1649, he drained a flagon of blood from one of his parishioners, and then pumped it into another parish volunteer.

At his trial for murder, Reverend Potter protested that *had* his experiment worked, it would have been a jolly good idea. As a result, in 1650, a law was passed in England strictly forbidding "sanguine transfusions."

Sixteen years later, a Frenchman got the same idea. He used his cousin and a sheep. Both went into convulsions from what we now know is an immunological reaction. A law prohibiting blood transfusions was also passed in France.

For the next two centuries, there are no recorded attempts by gentlemen dabblers to meddle with transfusions.

Then, in 1900, an Austrian scientist, Karl Landsteiner, discovered the existence of blood types. This was the breakthrough needed for the safe transfusion of human blood.

The rest is history.

The rest of the speech goes on to cite the record of the Blood Center, the current and projected needs, and then to praise the efforts of volunteers collectively and by name. I can assure you that it was a wildly successful speech, and I used a lot of it in a different blood drive speech sometime later, having also turned up the fact that after the inauspicious beginnings of blood collection and transfusion in England, that nation saw the invention of the modern blood drive. Furthermore, the founder of the blood-collection movement was the brother of John Maynard Keynes. Little facts like these can be very useful.

In speeches such as these, you are limited only by the bounds of good taste.

13.2   And Now Introducing

Most of us have had occasion to sit through introductions of guest speakers that sounded like recitations of their résumés—where they were born, where they went to college, what they studied and published, whom they married, their clubs, boards, professional associations, etc.

You want to bring these people to life. If the introducer knows the person, try to elicit some personal reminiscence about the guest. If not, try to place the appearance in a context that will make the speaker particularly relevant to the audience. They are there to listen to this person for a good reason. Make sure that they understand the reason. If there's no personal connection, call up people who do know the speaker, or at least know about him.

Sometimes, the guest your speaker is going to introduce is an august personage, important not so much for who he is but what he is. In such cases, you may be stuck for something noteworthy about the guest, but you can write most entertainingly about his job.

I once had to write an introduction for a vice-president of the United States. Let's face it. Most vice-presidential candidates aren't chosen for their star qualities. They generally display a degree of talent, charisma, and accomplishment a notch or two below their senior running mate. This is true with most cabinet secretaries, too, at least at the beginning of their terms. Destiny lies ahead of these people.

In the case of my introduction of a (now) former vice-president, I chose a history of the office of the vice-presidency. Dull? Maybe. After all, if vice-presidential candidates are chosen deliberately not to outshine the president, they may only get their moment after a national tragedy; if all goes well, they may make very little impression on history. So the history of the vice-presidency is dull, unless you find the theme of obscurity fascinating in its own right, and if you don't, you shouldn't be a speechwriter, because this is the kind of little paradox that makes the profession come to life.

There's very little written about the achievements of vice-presidents who never succeed to the top office, but since some of them have done so, you can resurrect their earlier careers by working down from the top. The *Oxford Book of Presidential Anecdotes* provided all the material I needed. My favorite story was about Calvin Coolidge. When he was the VP, there was no official vice-presidential residence, so he lived in a Washington hotel. One night it caught fire, and he was obliged to stand outside in his bathrobe while the firemen went about their task.

When the fire was out, Coolidge approached the fire chief and asked if he could return to his room. The chief asked, "Who are you?"

"I'm the vice-president," Coolidge replied.

Hearing this, the chief gave his consent, then called Coolidge back.

"Vice-president of what?"

"Of the United States."

To which the chief said, "Then you'd better stay out. I thought you were vice-president of the hotel."

Each profession has characteristics that are worth exploring. Don't miss your opportunity to have fun and try to avoid the easy way out. What passes for cleverness in some quarters may be tiresome in others.

Herbert Stein, a distinguished economist in and out of government and academia, wrote a very good article some years ago in *Fortune* on the indignities inflicted on members of his profession when they are introduced.

It's a good bet that over half of them [people who are introducing economists] will use one, two, or even three of the following lines.

1. "Economics is the dismal science." This was a favorite line of President Nixon's early in his administration, perhaps because that was the only thing his speechwriter on economics, William Safire, knew about the subject. As time passed, both the president and his speechwriter learned more and gave up the cliché.

2. "As President Truman said, 'I wish I had a one-armed economist, so that he wouldn't say on the one hand and on the other hand.' " If that was what Truman wanted, he was wrong. . . . It is the president's role to decide what to do when no one "knows" what to do. It is the role of the president's economic advisers to tell him of the options and of the *possible* consequences of his decision. It is their role to tell him that on the one hand this might happen and on the other hand that might happen.

3. "Economists never agree." This is sometimes buttressed with a quotation attributed to George Bernard Shaw that if all the economists were laid end to end, they would not reach a conclusion.

Stein says that in fact, most economists agree on most things. If there is any categorical disagreement, it is between economists and noneconomists.

He advises that "there is no need to introduce an economist with a joke. It is done, presumably, to put the audience in a tolerant frame of mind, but that doesn't last. It only succeeds in irritating the economist, who then feels obliged to continue with other jokes. If the convention wants jokes, it should engage Art Buchwald. Economists should not be expected to tell jokes for one-fourth of Buchwald's fee."

13.3 Welcome, Welcome, Welcome

A welcome is more than just shaking hands and saying hello. You can do that at the door. You establish the mood for the proceedings. You let the audience know why they are there and why you are there. Speechwriting is often a matter of presenting serious subjects with a light touch, balancing information with entertainment.

13.4 Dinner Is Served

The chairperson of a fund-raising dinner is under a solemn obligation to treat the cause with the gravity it deserves, without forgetting that people have paid a lot of money and expect to have a good time for it. But put everything in its place. You can assume that when people have visited the bar, milled around, and shaken hands with their friends and colleagues, it's best to give them a chance to get some food in their stomachs before they have anything else to drink. So probably the best thing to do initially is to welcome them, establish the mood, and let them get on with their dinner, and wait till after they're done eating before you start entertaining them. Here's an example of a good, functional pre-dinner welcome:

> Thank you, Bishop Goodnessme. I'm Jolly Goodfellow, chairman of this year's dinner.
>
> Welcome to the annual presentation of Manhattan College's De La Salle Award. Tonight is something of a double-barreled occasion. We're also celebrating the 300th anniversary of the founding of the Brothers of the Christian Schools. Fittingly, the De La Salle Medal is named after the founder of that order, John Baptiste de la Salle, the patron saint of teachers.
>
> Even for a saint, that's got to be a tough job.
>
> De La Salle Award winners have uniformly been men and women of strong ideals—with the grit and determination to see that their convictions take some concrete form.
>
> You could almost say that they are present-day examples of the kind of determined men who built the order and its schools.
>
> The four Christian Brothers who came to America alone in 1853 had that combination of pluck and conviction. They built a small school in the wilds of upper Manhattan and persevered until they got forty-five pupils.

Today Manhattan College has a modern campus in Riverdale and an enrollment of some five thousand.

It is still run by religious brothers who have the vigor and sinew of their predecessors—but today it takes more than determination to run a college. It takes the loyalty of alumni, the energy of the community, and the strong dedication of business leaders like my friend, and tonight's honored guest, Lance Trueblood.

But most of all, it takes the staunch support of men and women of goodwill—like all of you here tonight.

Now, to show you how much I appreciate your efforts on behalf of Manhattan College, I'm going to stop talking and let you enjoy your dinner.

13.5   Presenting an Award

When you are presenting an award, you aren't just recognizing an individual, you are also honoring an ideal. You have to remind people of those ideals and the stringent criteria that were used to select the honoree. Make your audience feel that they are part of something important. They put their time and money into the cause. You want them to keep on doing it, and they won't if you don't remind them to take it seriously.

But that doesn't mean you have to be all work and no play. That opportunity can come when you're actually talking about the recipient, who has, after all, many facets. Give the audience a feel for who the person is and the nature of their contribution. In many cases, of course, the person is chosen because they have raised a lot of

121

money, or their company has raised a lot of money. But you don't want to be that crass. In those cases, search for an odd angle.

The following is the post-prandial continuation of the De La Salle remarks, recounted above.

Discovering that the De La Salle Award is named after the patron saint of teachers gave me an idea. If teachers are allotted a special saint to look after them, don't we businessmen also need someone to intercede in heaven for us?

When I asked Brother Stephen about this, he suggested that under today's economic conditions, maybe we should pray to Saint Jude.

Brother Malcolm, on the other hand, suggested Saint Anthony, who has a good record for recovering losses.

When I called the New York Diocese, they informed me that a lot of my favorite saints were demoted a few years back. For example, Saint Christopher is no longer on the liturgical calendar, but his medals still outsell American cars.

Maybe heaven is trying to tell us something.

Finally, I asked my good friend Lance whom he's been praying to all these years. I thought that by finding out which saints have been looking after him, I could penetrate the secret of his success. Here's what I discovered.

He started his career with a Bachelor of Science degree from the University of Texas. Obviously, Saint Albert, the patron saint of scientists, got him through school.

He went on for a Master's in Chemical Engineering at MIT with the help of Saint Ferdinand of Spain, who looks after engineers. The good saint also got him a job as a student engineer at Rancid Oil and made sure that he moved up rapidly through the ranks.

In 1971, Lance and Saint Ferdinand took over as chairmen of the board, and the next year they became CEO.

This past fall, they both took normal retirement. I might add that Lance is in great shape, but I imagine that Saint Ferdinand might be a bit tired.

On his way to the top, our distinguished guest also became the object of other saints' patronage.

Saint Cecilia sponsored him at the Metropolitan Opera, where he's a board member. And Saint Luke put in a good word for him with the board of Presbyterian Hospital.

Rumor has it that Saint Bernardine, who takes an interest in communications, is responsible for his directorship at GTE.

I haven't been able to discover which saint put him up for the Conference Board. He may have made that one on his own.

I know personally that Saint Andrew has spent years trying to improve Lance's golf game, when he should have been helping me with mine.

Tonight, he's going to have another high-level saint to look after him. And now, as the saints go marching in, I'd like to introduce our honored guest.

13.6 Accepting an Award

My favorite acceptance speech was given by Pete Rose (before his gambling problems made him a bad example for our youth), who was honored at a big fund-raising

123

dinner. He earned the award because he was Pete Rose. No one ever pretended he was a great humanitarian. Having been cited in a flattering speech by J. Peter Grace, chairman of W. R. Grace, Rose said, "Mr. Grace told me he was a hurdler in college and he showed me how big his calf muscles were. Hell, I'd be strong too if I had to carry all that money to the bank." A Rose is a Rose, and no one ever said he was humble.

But most of us are, and we have to carry it off in a style that is sincere, without being obsequious. Academy Award and Grammy winners, who surely have the most radioactive egos on our planet, have done their best to give humility a bad name. Still, recognition is sweet for all of us, and when it comes, it should be accepted with whatever combination of humility and pride the honored personages really feel; no one is going to review their speeches the way television critics review the Oscars.

When people ask me for help in drafting speeches expressing their gratitude, I try to figure out whether the award is for some real personal achievement or because their company contributed the most money to the cause. If it's truly personal, I usually tell them that I have very little to add to what they have to say for themselves. If the achievement is personal enough, their first-hand knowledge of what they've done, and their sincere appreciation, make for a better speech than I can ever write.

If not, then the speech should really be about the cause. Sometimes executives commit their companies to causes for intensely personal reasons, and those reasons can be mentioned, although without becoming maudlin.

Sometimes an executive may get involved with a cause more as a matter of public relations than real personal interest. There's a story about one hardheaded captain of industry who served on the board of the Metropolitan Opera company and grew impatient with the imperious attitude of the legendary Sir Rudolf Bing. Finally, this executive couldn't take it anymore. He told Bing and the rest of the board, "I've figured out how the Met can stop losing so much money. We should do three shows a day."

Bing sniffed, "But no opera company in the world does three shows a day."

"Why not?" our iconoclast asked. "They do it in burlesque."

There's no record of this executive ever being given a testimonial dinner by the Met.

I'm sure that there are plenty of ballet board members who would really rather be out playing golf than watching people dancing in their pajamas. Yet these people are regularly given awards. In such cases, the speech can be about the millions of people who made it possible, and only incidentally one's deep honor at having been recognized for one's own contribution.

13.7 The Flip Side of Flippancy

You can't always afford to be flippant about the subject matter. Blood from the donor's point of view has its light and serious sides (from the donee's side it's a matter of life and death.) The vice-presidency has its light and serious sides. After all, one VP said that the office didn't amount to "a bucket of warm spit." An image like that gives you a certain amount of license. And whatever they are being paid, many economists know both sides of a joke.

But there are other subjects that challenge our capacity for whimsy. It's hard to give the lighter side of cancer. However, if you have had it, you can get away with it. I once heard Otto Graham, all-time great quarterback for the Cleveland Browns, who had conquered colonic cancer, give a funny and inspiring speech at an American Cancer Society fund-raiser about the convenience of using a colostomy bag.

Still, even if you can't be funny and uplifting because of your experience, it doesn't mean a grim subject has to result in a dull speech. You may not be able to make jokes about the cause, but if your speaker is helping raise money by sponsoring a dinner, you can have him extol the hard work of the fund-raising committee, and make jokes about the work behind the scenes that went into putting the event together. Speakers who have lent their names to a cause (and donated both money and staff time) can show how important they are by simultaneously deprecating their own role and elevating the people who actually did the work.

When it comes time to actually talk about the cause, you can make a comfortable shift. "But all this levity

126

doesn't diminish the seriousness of our purpose tonight." Here again, research is the key. Find ways to inform your audience. Use statistics, high-minded quotations, and heartrending stories that instruct and inspire.

13.8 Rallying the Troops

Most companies sponsor awards, dinners, company outings, and other occasions to bolster morale. A cynic would say it's cheaper than giving raises. A more ingenuous soul would observe that there are factors that make a greater contribution to job satisfaction than just money, and that most of us derive greater self-esteem from our jobs than we do from any other aspect of our lives. It's sheer arithmetic. Assuming you get eight hours of sleep per night, five days a week you spend more of your waking time commuting and working than you do at anything else. It helps to like it.

For management, it pays to stroke employees, and if you are writing a speech for the troops, it demands as much attention, creativity, and good humor as any external speech. The best ones are a mix of entertainment and a fresh expression of the larger common purpose.

Here's a beauty written for a large chemical company:

Someone sent Dr. Harold Morowitz, a molecular biophysics professor at an Ivy League college, a birthday card that said, "According to biochemists, the materials

127

that make up the human body are only worth ninety-seven cents." Dr. Morowitz gets annoyed when people depreciate themselves. He took a catalogue from a biochemical supply firm and computed the cost of the human body at current market prices. While some ingredients are fairly cheap—hemoglobin and albumin are only three dollars a gram—others show the influence of inflation. Acetatekinase is $8,860 a gram, bradykinin $12,000 a gram, and a follicle-stimulating hormone $4.8 million a gram. The street price of prolactin is $17.5 million a gram. By averaging all these constituents, Dr. Morowitz arrived at a figure of $6,000,015.44 for a medium-sized human being.

His figures prove that we are all six-million-dollar men! I was delighted when I heard this story—and all set for this evening's proceedings—until I read some bad news.

A Swiss research firm had announced the discovery of a cheap laboratory method to produce human interferon, a virus-fighting substance in our blood that is prohibitively expensive.

Do you know what that means? Thanks to science and technology, which are leading to cheaper ways of producing expensive chemicals, we're all being marked down to ninety-seven cents again.

While this turn of events shows that the human body won't be worth as much in the future, it does demonstrate one thing. That the human brain is priceless.

That's why we're here tonight. To honor the human brain. Your brains to be exact. Judging from the research accomplishments we are celebrating, I'm convinced that we have at least six billion dollars' worth of gray matter right here in this room. Only we're not selling. We believe your achievements are an indication of even greater things to come.

Look at the fields in which we've experienced breakthroughs, or product and process improvements: aerospace technology, cancer drugs, polymer catalysts, antihypertensives, pesticide formulations, antiperspirant production, resin coatings, sutures, enzyme inhibitors, calorimeters, antiasthmatics, vitamin compression, and a spectrum of cost-reducing and material-conserving innovations.

I predict that in the next few years, thanks to your six-billion-dollar brains, we will become a six-billion-dollar company. We've got a lot of good things in the works. And we've got a lot to be proud of.

Innovation is the key to our future. Too often we talk about innovation in terms of scientific abstractions, or of budget. So much so, I think, that we tend to lose sight of what is really involved. We forget that sutures make operations possible; that antihypertensives save people from strokes; that anticancer agents prolong life; and that antiasthmatics allow people to breathe.

Our animal health products and pesticides do increase world food production. Thanks to them, we enjoy abundant meat, ripe vegetables, and unspoiled fruit. Our chemicals contribute to the strength and safety of everyday materials—from airplanes to automobiles, from housing to furnishings.

Our lifestyle products make modern living clean and pleasurable. Consider how our free time has increased through the convenience and utility of products like synthetic fibers and laminates.

Science has made our way of life possible. That's why we're celebrating here tonight. But science is also a

129

serious business. Everything we do isn't going to yield a new product. The real key to scientific discovery is being able to say, "It doesn't work." It takes courage to say that—and not be too terribly discouraged. We can't delude ourselves as other people can. The truth always comes out in the lab. Tonight, while we are honoring people who have succeeded, we should save a little gratitude for those of our friends who ended up in blind alleys.

It was hard on them, but they saved us a trip. There's a big gap between the rapid pace of basic science and its application to human problems. With all of our new knowledge in the biological sciences, we still have formidable diseases with no real cures, and we are discovering harmful, long-term effects of many chemicals previously believed safe.

Your job is to use the mass of new scientific knowledge in ways that will be beneficial and safe for human beings. The work may be long and hard before really important applications can be made.

Consider the staggering amount of research to subdue infectious diseases. Generations of researchers exhausted their careers on the problem before the breakthrough of antibiotics.

By building on the vast foundation of science—hard won through previous research—you scientists have been able to come up with new cures, new chemicals, new products and processes.

Science itself asks no questions and provides no solutions; it is the human mind that asks questions and solves problems. The opportunities are limitless. I think that's what makes being a research scientist for a corporation exciting. You have the opportunity to apply the whole body of scientific knowledge to the solution of our most pressing human problems.

Not only this company, but the whole world is relying on you—our six-billion-dollar men and women. What can we expect from you? And what do you need to continue to provide more achievements of the high caliber we are celebrating tonight?

I've been a laboratory chemist and I hope I understand your needs. As I see it, you want the facilities and the equipment to do your jobs properly and creatively. This company is committed to providing them. We've budgeted $500 million for research and development.

Second, I think you want the encouragement of your superiors and of the officers of your company. Let me assure you that we believe in you and that you have our wholehearted support. And finally, you want recognition of the importance of your work by your colleagues and by your company.

Tonight you have both. Your company is proud of you. And your colleagues honor you. We have great faith in what you will accomplish in the future. We think you are worth your weight in gold.

Which leads me to another news story I read. It was an unverified account of how two Russian scientists, working in a nuclear laboratory near Siberia's Lake Baikal, accidentally managed to make gold through particle bombardment of lead. More importantly, the Russian scientists are said to have gone on with this surprising alchemy and to make it at the cost of six hundred dollars an ounce.

While American experts do not deny that the Russians, who are ahead of us in fusion research, could have produced gold—they say it is unlikely. They also say one way to tell if the story is true is to watch the price of lead.

Well, I did. Lead is rising. I don't know how much credence to put in this story. I just want to ask you, if any of you do accidentally turn up a way to produce gold— out of lead or anything else, except maybe platinum— please give me a call. Collect. Any hour of the day or night. Thank you.

Section 6

SPECIAL PROBLEMS

Most of this book is concerned with the mainstream speaker and the mainstream audience. But this is a fast-moving society. American speakers have to address non-American audiences; American companies hire non-native English speakers; foreign speakers address American audiences; people of diverse talents populate corporations. In this section, I'm going to talk about some situations I've encountered outside the plain-vanilla problem of speech-writing.

CHAPTER
14

Writing for a Member of the
Opposite Sex

A friend of mine (woman) had to write a speech for an executive (man) who had to pay tribute to the cause of women in industry. It had to acknowledge the contradictions without apology or chagrin. It had to be serious without being solemn. It had to be good-humored without being flippant. The frame of reference on the place of women in corporate America had to make sense for the speaker—it would take an exceptional male CEO to convincingly cite any prominent feminist writers.

This is the solution:

> I would like to welcome you to the National YWCA's first tribute to women in international industry.
>
> And it's about time.
>
> Remember the old movies, those marvelous films of the thirties and forties that showed career women— Katherine Hepburn, Rosalind Russell, Joan Crawford— striding about in tailored suits with shoulders so padded they could have played for Notre Dame? Executive

women, as we saw them on the screen, had an unreal glamour. They were featured in hundreds of films. But we knew these were only movies. Life was not like that.

Still, professional women had a fascination for all of us. Of course, I am talking about role models—and those 35-millimeter career women fulfilled the fantasies of an entire generation. When I asked one of my women managers what had inspired her to aim high, she admitted that as a child she had been a movie fan. "I never learned to type well," she confessed, "because I always wanted to be like Rosalind Russell in *Take a Letter, Darling*, and have a male secretary who looked like Fred McMurray."

Well, I've got to hand it to her. She found a model for success—even if it was a celluloid one.

At [name of company] today, we are proud of our growing force of professional women. They are a vital part of the corporation. But, I am sorry to say, we have not done as well employing male secretaries. Paul Newman, Burt Reynolds, and Robert Redford all turned down jobs in our typing pool.

What I am saying is that role models are important influences for success. And that is what these awards are all about. We are here tonight to recognize real live achievement.

And so on. . . .

I'd like to elaborate a bit on this business of gender. Becky Morris, the author of the passage just quoted, has remarked on how few women she has written for over the years—a function of the percentage of senior women executives there are in the companies she has worked for.

In fact, while she herself is an ardent feminist, her work has been attacked because she has succeeded in adopting the male voice so totally. One of her speakers was once accused of sexism for quoting from *Diamonds Are a Girl's Best Friend*.

Women can write for men and men can write for women (as I have done). But there are differences in what male and female speakers can plausibly say. The following is a passage about the prospects for women at the top levels of management in retailing, written by a woman for a woman:

> First: It's important to give women the same training and opportunity as men. This means those tough special assignments and travel duties. Don't assume women will refuse such jobs. Women today are alert to the time, dedication, and risk-taking needed to develop the seasoning required to enter senior management.
>
> Second: When the timing is right, management must have the courage to give qualified women a shot at the top jobs. When the only prerequisite is talent, women deserve the same chance as men to succeed or fail.
>
> Third, and perhaps most important: It's time for management to take a more supportive attitude toward the aspirations of women managers and actively encourage them to "go for" the challenges of senior management.
>
> The reason I stress this point is that many women today still aren't comfortable aspiring to top management levels. They are reluctant to reveal the kind of ambition we so often admire in male executives. There are many ways to explain this, but one of the most accepted theories today is the fear-of-success syndrome—

first identified by Martina Horner, ex-president of Radcliffe College. Ms. Horner maintains that many women hold themselves back from success because they are afraid of the negative consequences they associate with intellectual achievement, such as perceived loss of femininity and social attractiveness.

Such attitudes are still blocking the progress of women. I suspect that everyone in this room can think of at least one qualified woman who hasn't reached senior management simply because she hasn't "gone for it" the way her male counterparts would.

This speech could have been written by a man. But I doubt whether any man would have delivered it as written. The same words in the mouth of a man would probably provoke accusations that "you men are telling us women what to do; don't fight our battles for us." Men can't be seen to be critical of women on the same terms as women can be self-critical. And Becky Morris would agree with me. It won't do for a speaker to claim that "some of my best speechwriters are women."

So whether the issue is gender, subject matter, race, creed, or color, the message for you is that you have to keep the voice appropriate for the speaker. You don't want your speakers to be hung for their politics, you want them to be hung for their ideas . . . wait a minute, let me put that another way. You don't want your speakers to rise or fall for reasons extraneous to the larger message. You want to help them make their case.

CHAPTER
15

*American Speakers; Foreign
Audiences*

An American executive I know lived abroad for twenty years. Unfortunately, his postings seem to have covered too wide a range of territory. He delivered a speech in Spanish, and at the end, his host asked politely if he could supply a copy of the original text so that it could be translated into Spanish.

The lesson I draw from this is a heartening one for speechwriters who write in English—namely, that polyglot executives are unlikely to put us out of business.

But when writing for Americans in the mother tongue for delivery abroad, we have to be even more careful than we are with the domestic product. The gaps between what will wash in different parts of the United States are nothing compared to what we're up against in crossing the water. I'm married to an Englishwoman, and believe me I know.

But if England and America are two countries separated by a common tongue, as George Bernard Shaw tells us, it's a far greater problem when speaking in English to non-English speakers. One ugly American decided that the key to bridging American and Japanese differences was humor. He thought that he could surmount the cultural, racial, and business obstacles between the two countries with jokes. He instructed his writer to load the script with one-liners, and went off to Tokyo. Speaking in English, he paused between paragraphs while a translator rendered his words into Japanese.

Well, Bob Hope never had a better audience. They laughed right on cue, and he stepped down from the podium convinced that he was going to make a real advance for United States–Japanese relations and for his company. Until he spoke to a Japanese-speaking American, who told him what had happened. The translator had said, "This American fool obviously thinks he's a really funny guy. We don't want to be rude, so when I tell you to laugh, laugh."

Therein lie the limitations of doing business in the global economy. English may be the international language of business. Non–U.S. executives and other eminences may speak terrific English and understand it better, but you can't afford to be too colloquial. After all, there's American English and there's English English and there's Oxford-and-Cambridge English English, and Australian English, and so on—your audiences may have mastered one and not the others. You have to strive for clarity, perhaps at the expense of some of the techniques that we've dealt with earlier in this book. It's to your advantage, however, that your audience will likely be that much more attentive than a native audience.

That's not to say that you should ignore the tricks of the trade. If anything, the kind of research we talked about earlier in this book will be much more important. If your audience sees that you have gone out of your way to learn something about them, their culture, customs, history, and local business conditions, they will appreciate it a great deal. Try no less than with any other audience to relate big themes to the particulars of their particular marketplace.

It's quite acceptable to use a few rudimentary words of their language to ingratiate your speaker, but make sure you get them right. Dick Cavett says that he tries to practice his Japanese every chance he gets, but when he asked for his check in a sushi restaurant, the waitresses burst out laughing. Apparently he erred in the length of the vowel, and asked for an enema instead.

Business history is replete with examples of this kind of thing. There's the story that when Chevrolet marketed its Nova in Latin American countries, it didn't sell. In English, *nova* is associated with the Latin word for new. In Spanish, the word for new is *nueva*; *no va* means "doesn't go." Then there's the time Pepsi tried to use its slogan "Come alive" in Taiwan, which translated as "makes your ancestors rise from the dead." With the opening of Eastern Europe to Western investment, there was the translation of the term "blue-chip corporation" into "corporation that manufactures blue chips."

Don't assume that what you think is acceptably funny will go over in a foreign setting. Don't tell *mañana* jokes in Mexico, for example, as someone I know once did.

15.1 Foreign Speakers; American Audiences

You can't write the same speech for a foreign-born speaker that you wrote for an American. You must acknowledge the differences. While the message can be substantially the same as that aimed at Americans, the way in which it is approached may be fundamentally different. Your job as the speechwriter is to mediate between the sensibilities and cultures of speaker and audience.

The normal strictures about complexity of words, phrases, and sentence structures apply doubly here. You can't afford to get careless or cute.

The sensibility has to fit. I have had trouble writing for certain Asian-born executives, even when they have been raised and educated in the United States; their style was too matter-of-fact for me. They weren't out to ingratiate themselves with their audiences in any way other than plain courtesy. They were more out to inform than to persuade, and since their knowledge of their subject was a great deal deeper than mine would ever be, it was easier for them to just dictate what they wanted to say to their secretaries, or to get their closest aides, who knew them minutely, to do it for them. I'm too much of a generalist. You can't win 'em all.

On the other hand, the continental Europeans I've dealt with have been much more amenable to my help, and much gamer about using informal material that was likely to ingratiate them with American audiences. Likewise, American audiences appreciate the efforts of an English-as-second-language speaker. A German I used to know liked to mark each anniversary, promotion, transfer, or retirement in his division with a doggerel poem, and he bravely battled his way through some of the most tortured rhymes in history. People loved it.

I once wrote a speech for a Dutchman who noted that the Dutch were (at that time) the largest foreign investors in the United States economy and vice versa. Equating this with the notion of "Dutch treat" went over well with a California audience at a time when foreign investment in the United States was deemed more of a threat than as a necessity, as it is now.

You are the arbiter of the American mind for your foreign-born speakers. Help them. Educate them. Get them to stretch.

CHAPTER
16

Dyslexia

I've found that dyslexia is fairly common in business people. Very smart people affected by it have ways of compensating and often develop a drive that can take them far in business and public life. I know a number of dyslexics in fields such as architecture, graphic design, and engineering, where spatial perception and the facile manipulation of symbols are more important than the ability to read quickly.

Still, when dyslexics become executives, they have to rely on the written word. A speechwriter may not get much work out of them. Rather than risk the possibility that an act of "dog" will cause them great embarrassment in reading a speech at the podium, they compensate by becoming excellent, energetic extemporaneous speakers.

However, sometimes they will call on you to write a speech that they can study at their own pace and internalize, either memorizing it, or picking up a feel for the tone, message, and style and recapitulating it in their own words (sometimes with the help of outlines, bullet points, or pictures).

(Some speech coaches suggest that *all* speakers abandon the written text, and use, instead, visual cues and pictures to help them through a presentation. They feel that the ingenuousness and spontaneity of such a performance more than compensates for the stilted perfection of a script-bound speaker. But much to the relief of all of us pro speechwriters, plenty of speakers need us. And furthermore, as one PR maven pointed out, "If one picture is worth a thousand words, draw me the Gettysburg Address.")

When working with dyslexics, write even more carefully than usual. Don't count on their ability to quickly grasp the sense or meaning of what you think are ordinary constructions. If there are to be rehearsals, and there certainly should be, get yourself invited. Listen to the reading. You will discover ambiguity you never suspected.

I once heard a fellow deliver a line something like, "The power of diplomacy used to reside with the executive branch." In his reading, the phrase *used to*, instead of referring to the past, sounded more like a verb in a subordinate clause, as in "mashed potatoes, *used to* stick peas on a knife, are practical as well as delicious." Even

145

repeated explanations couldn't untrack his reading, and so the line was rewritten.

Hang in there. The speaker needs you to help him think through a problem, but he has to have it presented to him in terms he can use. You will learn a lot, too.

CHAPTER
17

Technical Matters

17.1 Writing for Delivery with Accompanying Slides

I put this section just after dyslexia because if dyslexia is an obstacle some speakers must overcome, then writing for slides is an obstacle for writers. Slides are the revenge of the experts. They write the slides, and you have to write from them. Slides heavy on text are really the notes people might take in a dull lecture. I say, just give us the notes and let us go get a drink.

Sometimes, as in business reviews, there are more important things for speakers to do than just be interesting. I happen to think that the professional writer's touch would add something to these occasions, especially if there's extra money in it.

If you must write to these miserable slides, try to stretch the speaker. Add some images, ideas, analogies— anything to keep yourself, the speaker, and the audience awake.

Sometimes you are expected to use slides even in more public settings. These slides should add something that you can't provide in the text. Long lists of numbers belong on a screen, not in your speaker's mouth. Let the speaker interpret the numbers and let the numbers speak for themselves.

If you have access to picture research or original art, expand on the slides with drawings, cartoons, photographs. You can use them to get a few laughs.

17.2 The Script

Different speakers like different presentation formats. Some like to use index cards. I suppose it makes them feel masterful to haul out a few discreet cards and pretend to speak from notes. But what a pain in the neck. You can't push a button and have the thing print out. They have to be typed on a typewriter, of all things, and a large-type machine at that.

Luckily for you, however, with the emphasis on efficiency and cost saving so pervasive in modern business, there aren't many execs left who will dare to utilize such retrograde technology. And besides, you can't put a long speech on cards. The stack would be so thick that the bulge would spoil the line of the speaker's suit.

17.3   Type Styles and Margins

Modern word processors can provide a wonderful array of type styles and sizes, to suit any speaker's taste and eyesight. You can experiment to get just the right one to suit your speaker. Big versions, sixteen- or eighteen-point, of regular typewriter type are easier to read than anything fancy.

When I submit a script for comment, I often run it in regular type but with margins on all sides that pretty much indicate a delivery length of a minute per script page. A double-spaced page with one-inch margins, left-right and top-bottom, is about two minutes a page. Two-inch margins, left, right, top, and three on the bottom, will cut the word count in half, and with it the time per page. This helps the speaker calculate the pace of delivery and provides him with plenty of room to write his own notes and comments.

If you want to be really tricky, give it to the speaker in the one-minute-per-page format and to his staff in the two-minute version. This sometimes discourages the staff from making wholesale changes.

If you don't have a current word-processing program and a nice laser printer, you can still produce a decent performing script. Speech type on the cheap would be all capital letters typed with triple-spacing.

17.4   Phrasing

Some coaches tell their pupils that normal sentences
and paragraphs make it hard for the eye to follow and-
difficult for the speaker to give an engaging performance
because he's too busy looking
down.
Instead,
the writer
breaks each sentence
into phrases that are
easy to spot, and
comfortable units
for the breath capacity
of the
average speaker.

It is, of course,
a
pain in the neck
for the writer,
or for the secretary,
who must actually
do the work.

Thank God
for the word processor.

150

17.5 Adding Visual Cues to the Script

Underlining and other visual cues may be added ahead of time either by the speaker or the writer to help with emphasis and other interpretive details. It pays to be aware of things like this and to be able to suggest them to speakers if they ask for help. However, few speakers seem to arrive spontaneously at the idea that they need such help. Generally, they need training from some pro who recommends a system. Then, if you're lucky, the speaker will send you for a couple of days of training from the teacher so that you can learn it, too.

17.6 Titles

All of what I've written so far is aimed at the delivery of speeches. If, however, the speech is likely to be published, it generally needs a title. You can always say "Remarks by J. Sheldon Snodgrass, Chairman and CEO of American Depilatory Trust Company." If you're going for a title, there are several kinds. One is purely descriptive. "The Dangers of Highly Leveraged Transactions"; "Corporations and the Environment"; "Problems in the Insurance Industry."

You see titles like these and you know what you're getting. And they can be the best kind, if you're intent on making sure that your position is accepted as part of the public discussion of a particular problem.

Others are more evocative. They will intrigue even people without a natural interest in the subject. Walter Wriston's "The Independent Man and the Transference Machine" is one. Another was "Grandpa, What Was a Bank?" Or "The Great Whale Oil Syndrome." These refer to ideas within the speech.

I like to use titles that evoke the metaphorical hook of the speech itself, and metaphors that are strong enough to carry a speech generally have some powerful phrases associated with them. "Three Yards and a Cloud of Dust" was a good one for a speech about credit cards that used football as a theme.

If the speech is too poetic, of course, you lose the chance of grabbing the people whose interest is most immediate, so it doesn't hurt to use a descriptive subhead. Wordplays on familiar phrases, like many of the subheads in this book, can also give the title an extra dimension.

17.7   Coaching Your Speaker

People have urged me to give advice on how to help speakers prepare for their performance. The most important thing you can do is help them achieve ease with the text, to negotiate nuances and phrasing. The best way to do this is to read the text aloud yourself. When you discover where you run out of breath, rewrite the difficult bits. You will also learn why things mean what they do, and where they are vague or ambivalent. You can strengthen weak passages. Your own private performance will also equip you to answer the speaker's questions about the text.

With any luck, your speaker will have time for a read-through. You can rewrite to accommodate his idiosyncrasies of breath, phrasing, and demeanor.

Keep in mind that a good speaker looks at his audience, to the people in it; at their eyes, not at some neutral body part that can't look back. When a speaker keeps his shy eyes firmly on the audience's chests or shoulders, it comes across. If he is looking at their eyes, on the other hand, it animates the delivery. He's trying to convince those people out there, and he should spend at least a sentence or two on individuals. Avoiding eye contact is deemed to indicate a furtive character. Not very convincing. In rehearsal, try to engage the speaker's eyes. Get him to speak to you. It's a shortcut to confidence.

Many speech coaches have exercises, mantras, and other little rituals that they urge on their clients to help them prime themselves physically for the speech. I once took an excellent course from Dorothy Sarnoff in which she taught a warmup that reflected her training in the theater, complete with diaphragmatic breathing and a little chant about believing in oneself. Besides diaphragmatic breathing, speech coaches advise systematic

153

clenching and relaxing of all your muscles, sticking out your tongue, deep breathing to relieve tension, projecting your voice great distances, vibrating your sinuses and the rest of your resonating apparatus, and on and on—all of them abbreviated versions of stage technique.

I must confess that I blanch at the thought of actually doing one of these warmups, which is probably one reason why I write speeches but very rarely give them.

I will say two things in favor of such regimes, however:

1) Having watched my wife give birth three times with the Lamaze method, I believe that all that puffing and blowing doesn't make childbirth hurt any less. But it gives a woman something to think about while waiting for the pain to end. Such exercises probably have a similar effect on speakers who follow them.

2) If you're not embarrassed to do these things while you're waiting to go on, you probably won't be embarrassed delivering your speech either, which will make it a better speech.

As for the delivery, you want the speaker to avoid reading straight from the script. This is a performance, and the most convincing performance acknowledges the audience. Eyes should have sharp focus. Tell the speaker to look people in the eyes. Even in a large auditorium, if the speaker avoids eye contact, looking at people's shoulders instead of their faces, it registers with the rest of the audience. A whole sentence, a whole thought, per individual audience member, is about right.

Conclusion

T HE end is the hardest part to write. A good speech is more than the sum of those parts that the speechwriter supplies. There are all the intangibles as well, starting with the personality and persona of the speaker and the character of the audience.

Writing speeches the way I have described is not the only way to write them, but it works.

Each speech is a problem waiting to be solved. Your first task is to sketch out the nature of the problem— whom you're writing for, both speaker and audience— then fill in the pieces of the puzzle through research and logic, and finally to put it to words. The words themselves should be suggestive, descriptive, and pithy, but above all, easy on the ear. Good speeches are not the most finely tuned pieces of writing. They can be expansive and repetitive, making a case in broad strokes, rather than terse and tightly reasoned. They should contain your *best* arguments, not necessarily *all* the arguments.

The division between the way you write speeches and the way you speak should be narrower than it is for essay writing, although with essays or speeches, the terror of the blank page is abject enough to maintain a decent market for us ghosts. Keep that terror in mind when you're writing. It's the basis of your empathy with the speaker. "There but for the grace of executive status go I." Help that speaker do his or her job by doing yours.

Have fun. Don't get self-important about your work. It will show up as pomposity in the speech. Try to keep an open mind about things. Very few subjects are so cut-and-dried that knowing both sides of the issues won't help you in making the case for only one side.

Read. Listen to the radio. Allow yourself to be bombarded by information. You never know when it will come in handy. There's always a need for new metaphors, new analogies, new ideas.

Bury your pride of authorship. Writer's block and speechwriting don't mix. You have to take chances. Most of us feel that it's easier to give advice, and to see the wisdom or folly of other people's actions, than it is to do what's right for ourselves. Speechwriting gives you the luxury of that kind of detachment. You're not writing in your own voice. Putting someone else on the line should be easier than putting yourself on it. Take advantage of that.

The worst argument against writing your own speeches is that it keeps people like me from gainful employment. But if you must write your own speeches, try to maintain the distance you would feel if you were writing for someone else. Don't put yourself on the line twice at the same time. You, too, can have fun.

APPENDIX
1

Putting It Together—
A Whole Speech

H ERE's a speech by Thomas P. Grumbly, president of Clean Sites, called "The Environment: The Issue of the Nineties" that moves deftly through the three parts of a speech, with transitions that are smooth and all but seamless:

> It's a great pleasure to be here. A few minutes ago I went through Central Park, and I'm happy to report that the grass is on its way back after being trampled to death during the Earth Day celebration a couple of weeks ago.
>
> It will be a while, however, before we get a final count on how many trees have been destroyed throughout the world in order to produce all the recent books and articles on the environment.
>
> As for tonight's proceedings, I've got some good news and some bad news. The good news is that I don't plan to give a long speech. This is that critical time in the day when the sun is long over the yardarm, and I'm well

aware that I'm the last remaining barrier between you and the bar.

The bad news is that I feel compelled to say something significant about Earth Day. Most of you are probably bored with it by now. Either that, or you're thoroughly exhausted from the efforts to devise ingenious ways for your companies or clients to capitalize on it.

Russell Baker has said that, on general principles, he is opposed to any issue where 85 percent of the American public agree. Other pundits—from George Will to Leonard Silk—have pointed out that the environment has now become a motherhood issue. In other words, just because everyone appears to agree, it doesn't follow that we're ready to make the hard choices to really get something done.

I can be just as skeptical as George Will. In fact, I begin to wonder about an issue any time Robert Redford calls a conference on it at his ski resort in Sundance, Utah. You may have read about that particular environmental summit. It occurred last summer. The participants included Carl Sagan, Jane Pauley, Tom Brokaw, the cartoonist Garry Trudeau, various United States senators and representatives, and several businessmen and American Indian chiefs. They even invited a Russian named Kakimbek A. Salykov, who is the People's Deputy of the Supreme Soviet Committee on Ecology and the Rational Use of National Resources.

But I also believe there was far more to Earth Day than celebrity glitz, political posturing, or—if you will pardon the expression—publicity stunts. In fact, years from now when people look back on Earth Day, 1990, it will be seen as one of those great watershed events—an event symbolizing a new American consensus on the environment, a consensus that, for the first time, included elected officials, American business, and the American people at the grass roots.

In this speech, a skeptical, worldly eye toward some of the sanctimonious and absurd elements of environmentalism underscores the seriousness and authority of the speaker. The argument is developed quite effectively, establishing the maturing of the environment as a political issue, presented as concisely and crisply as today's news (now yesterday's).

Despite mounting local concern for many years, the environment has emerged as a national political issue only recently. You'll remember that George Bush discovered the issue rather late in the 1988 campaign. His handlers read some polls and noticed the visual possibilities of Boston Harbor. Before that his environmental position was limited to somewhat enigmatic references to the "ethics of outdoor recreation."

Governor Dukakis's contribution to the environmental issue was equally opaque. He called for the creation of Certified Public Toxics Auditors—or CPTAs. Certified Public Toxics Auditors—with a clarion call like that you wonder why he wasn't elected.

Since then, several things have happened to bring the issue of the environment front and center. There was the *Exxon Valdez* spill, which brought stunning visual images of oil-soaked sea birds and otters into American living rooms. There has also been the phenomenon of global warming, which is the successor to nuclear winter. The ancient prophets said the world would end in fire

or ice. So global warming has the right apocalyptic ring
to it.

The next bit is key to this speaker's thesis; namely, that
corporations, so long the enemy to the cause of environmentalism, live in this world, too, and they know which
side of the bread is buttered with their self-interest.

But in addition, there are two long-term trends in public
attitudes that, in my view, have immense significance.
The first is the deep concern over the environment that
has taken hold at the grass roots throughout America.
The second is the willingness of corporations to assume
their share of responsibility for the environment.

Skipping ahead, the speech shows that the ordinary
people are in the vanguard on this issue, which means
that corporations and the government fail to follow at
their peril.

USA Today recently ran a story trumpeting the fact that
83 percent of Americans now fear for the environment. It
was part of the hype leading up to Earth Day. But the real
significance is that there was little new in the *USA Today*
poll result. Other pollsters have been finding a growing
concern over the environment for the last ten years.
    It's just that the national media and most Washington
politicians didn't notice. Our elected representatives
didn't notice because environmental problems can be
complex, and there are often no easy answers. The media
didn't notice because a local garbage dump doesn't have

nearly the visual possibilities of an oil spill in Alaska. The national media takes the view of Spiro Agnew: when you've seen one waste site you've seen them all.

But people living near these sites clearly take a different view. And that's why concern over the environment has been building—long before anyone mentioned the ozone layer or biodiversity in Brazil.

It also helps to have some vivid, evocative anecdotal material.

There's no question that we've made progress on some fronts in recent years. The Cuyahoga River in Cleveland doesn't catch fire anymore, and there's less lead in the air than there was ten years ago. But the problems that have proven more difficult—such as hazardous waste—have tended to be more visible. People can take evidence of them with their own senses.

They can also read about these problems in their local newspapers. You may have noticed that up until recently the local media have been far more active than the national media in covering the environment. They have been more attuned to people's concerns and fears. My all-time favorite local media story is one that appeared in the *Newark Star-Ledger* two years ago. It's a funny story, but also demonstrates just why so many people are so worried about the environment. Let me read parts of it to you.

The headline proclaims: "Giant Trash Pyramid Perils Jersey Water." Mr. Vito Turso, public affairs director of the New York Sanitation Department, is then quoted describing the Staten Island landfill at Fresh Kills, which has the potential of reaching fifty stories high. That would make it, says Turso with evident New York pride, "the highest artificial land mass on the East Coast." He says, "We're building the Grand Canyon of the East. We'll be dumping garbage upward, defying the laws of gravity."

According to Turso, "We are limited in space, horizontally, so we have no other choice but to go up vertically, as far as engineering knowhow can push it." But he goes on to note that this is "unproven technology," so we'll just have to "wait and see what happens." For example, one worst-case scenario is that "a landslide could bury the West Shore Expressway, one of the two main thoroughfares on Staten Island."

As you might expect, certain local officials are expressing alarm at this manmade wonder of a garbage heap. Over in the Meadowlands, solid-waste supervisor Christopher Dour says, "It is the most unbelievably disgusting sight I've ever seen." New York City Councilwoman Susan Molinari pronounced the following olfactory judgment on the site: "You can smell that dump a mile away."

The former mayor of this city has been immortalized by having the landfill named after him. New Jersey residents call it "Mount Koch."

This anecdote builds to a crescendo, or should I say a peak, at the same time that it introduces a crucial part of the argument, the role of the government in managing the environment.

In the midst of all this public outcry, you may ask, "Where are the regulators?" Well, it appears that the federal government has been getting ready to step in, but it is not the agency you might expect. According to the *Star-Ledger*, the Federal Aviation Administration has been looking into the matter. The FAA apparently requires an air-space study whenever a structure reaches an altitude of two hundred feet. The City of New York has inquired about these height restrictions, and the FAA has sent them the forms to fill out, but has not yet received them back.

Now, having established the context, the speech shifts to the crux of the discussion—that corporations are falling into place in the fight for a safer environment for the only reason that makes sense for them over the long term, their own commercial viability—and it analyzes why it is in their interests. It also shows why the rest of us should be relieved, whether that reason satisfies what the *Wall Street Journal* calls the "PC" (politically correct) standard or not. The point is reinforced with much vivid detail.

It's clear that we're now in a position to act on a broad front with the full resources of society. In a capitalist society, the term "full resources" means that corporate America is getting on board. They have decided that it's good business to help protect the environment and be part of the solution. Most of you know that better than I do. It's your job to look out for your companies and clients in the public arena, to read the polls and election returns, and to stay off *60 Minutes*.

Milton Friedman has a theory that the only duty of a corporation is to maximize profits for its shareholders. It must obey the law, and pay taxes imposed on it, but its essential business is to go about its business, and not be concerned with wider social obligations, which are the province of government and other institutions.

This is an eminently logical theory, but it makes no sense whatsoever when we look at today's corporations and the way they have become enmeshed in environmental issues. On March 24 last year, the *Exxon Valdez* steamed out into Prince William Sound with its huge cargo of oil. All of you know the story that followed.

It was a large-scale disaster and Exxon certainly deserves much of the criticism it has received. The company was ill-prepared to respond to the accident, much of the clean-up technology was out of date, and its initial public statements have been less than a tour de force in public relations.

But in all the hand-wringing over the *Exxon Valdez* affair, one significant point has been largely overlooked: Exxon did respond, and responded in a big way. In fact, the company has now spent more than a billion dollars in an effort to clean up the damage, and they're going to end up spending a lot more than that.

Exxon has had to take responsibility because there are now clear public expectations, as well as tough laws, which mean that companies—especially big companies—must assume responsibility. That is a big change and it has occurred in just the last twenty years. Such responsibility on the part of corporations would have been laughed at in the days of the robber barons, and was unheard of even at the time of the first Earth Day back in 1970. Those were more confrontational times. Some of those first Earth Day participants poured sewage on corporate carpets and destroyed automobiles with sledgehammers. Most corporations were not eager to participate in the celebration.

But times have changed. A whole slew of laws in the early 1970s—such as the Clean Air Act and Clean Water

Act—created new obligations for corporations. Today, corporations are being asked to undertake voluntary obligations. I'm sure that many of you are now struggling with the Valdez Principles. I'm going to stay away from that hornet's nest.

Let me just say that back in the bad old days, such a code would have been ludicrous because very few corporations would ever acknowledge any voluntary responsibility. Today, however, there are numerous examples of corporations acting on their own to help with the environment.

DuPont, for example, is phasing out production of chlorofluorocarbons because of the danger they do to the ozone layer.

Atlantic Richfield Company has announced that it will start selling a cleaner-burning gasoline that will reduce some auto emissions by up to 20 percent.

Dow Chemical has joined other chemical companies in a sixteen-million-dollar venture to provide recycled plastics to manufacturers.

Procter & Gamble Company is involved in recycling programs that take soiled diapers and turn them into compost, trash bags, park benches, and insulation.

Monsanto is voluntarily reducing its toxic air emissions by 90 percent, and has announced a goal of zero toxic emissions.

Last week Unocal announced a five-million-dollar program to buy seven thousand of the oldest and dirtiest-burning cars in Los Angeles, and then scrap them. When it comes to carbon monoxide, hydrocarbon, or nitrogen-oxide emissions, the older cars still on the road are by far the biggest offenders. So the quickest and least costly way to improve the air is to get rid of them. Unocal will be paying dinosaur owners seven hundred dollars each and giving them a one-month bus pass.

Skeptics are saying that all this concern on the part of corporations is nothing more than clever marketing, a kind of environmental pandering. The general response to that is: who cares about motives? If businesses are now taking responsibility only because it is in their own long-term self-interest, is there anything wrong with that? Milton Friedman notwithstanding, we have come a long way from the days when corporations were expected simply to obey the laws, and little else. We have come a long way from the days when the head of U.S. Steel could thumb his nose at the president of the United States, and the president—President Kennedy—would say that all businessmen are SOBs.

If I'm correct on the trends I've just described—and they seem to be there plain as day—then there is good reason for optimism on the environment. The politics of any problem are always the most difficult to solve. The politics—the big-picture politics—of the environment are falling into place. Two key elements—the force of public opinion and the attitudes and actions of corporations—are making themselves felt.

After a recitation of facts in support of the larger point, and the delineation of the change that has been wrought in attitudes toward environmentalism, the speech shifts to the beginning of the end, which consists of prescription and prophecy. A strong way to signal such a shift is to change from the declarative to the interrogative. Ask a good rhetorical question, and then answer it. The speaker has established himself as an expert; he now suggests some plausible rules of thumb; and he dismantles some of the common arguments advanced by the "can't do" school of antienvironmentalism. The wit with which they are given is gentle, and therefore unthreatening. The reasons for doing the "right" thing are here. They are the carrot. Yet the threats of media exposure and government action are right behind. They are the stick. This is a strong and compelling way to make a case.

The question is: How do we proceed from here? We have a big opportunity. How do we make sure that we don't blow it?

With all due respect and modesty, let me offer my own short list of voluntary principles for corporations and public-relations professionals.

The first is: Don't pander. There is already enough skepticism out there about the true motives of corporations. The *USA Today* poll shows that when it comes to solving environmental problems, people have even less confidence in corporations than they do in the federal government. In terms of trust, people rank themselves first, state and local governments second, the federal government third, and corporations fourth.

So if that carbonated drink you're marketing doesn't really come out of the ground, don't say it does. If your cereal doesn't prevent heart attacks, don't say it does. And if your trash bags don't degrade into soil, don't say they do.

Mobil may have made an honest mistake on those Hefty Bags, but a little checking would have shown that not only is there no sunlight beneath the surface of a dump, there is very little oxygen. I wouldn't want to try it, but a member of the New York Sanitation Department told me that if you dig down into the core of that Staten Island landfill you can find roast beef that you can eat.

The no-pandering rule also applies to corporate image advertising. Don't go overboard. Whenever I see an ad that equates a corporation with Mother Teresa, I'm reminded of Ralph Waldo Emerson's line: "The louder he talked of his honor, the faster we counted the spoons."

Corporate pledges like the Valdez Principles and the chemical industry's "Responsible Care" ad campaign are enlightened. They had better be true, too, because they won't be forgotten when the Clean Air Act reauthorization reaches the floor of the House of Representatives or when a community demands that a hazardous waste site be cleaned. Companies will—and should be—called on to walk the way they talk, especially when the message is emblazoned on full-page ads in the *New York Times*, *People* magazine, and hundreds of other publications.

The second rule is: Don't try to filibuster on the basis of theological concepts like cost-benefit analysis or risk assessment. When it comes to matters involving basic health and safety, the public is not impressed by arguments involving angels on the head of a pin.

Science is usually imprecise and tentative, but it's also true that we now know enough about various environmental risks to take action. We know how to reduce certain risks and there's little to be gained from going round and round on the subject. This same rule applies to that old standby—the loss-of-jobs argument. It's not clear to me that any environmental regulation has ever resulted in any net loss of jobs in this country. In fact, these regulations have created any number of public-affairs jobs—including yours and mine.

Third: Corporate America must recognize that the government—particularly the federal government—will play a strong role in solving our environmental problems. Most of these problems are not going to be solved by the *Fortune* 1000 acting as a thousand points of light, or by shoppers taking string bags to the super-market.

For one thing, there are too many tradeoffs. What do you do about the use of plastic materials in cars that make them lighter, more fuel-efficient, and less polluting, but that will also sit forever in a landfill, even when exposed to sunlight and oxygen? Or about disposable diapers? If we go back to the washable kind, we'll consume more energy and send more hydrocarbons out into the atmosphere. These issues have to be decided through the political process.

We're also not about to send a corps of community volunteers out to clean up a toxic waste site, and it's not fair to ask a corporation to assume the cost and legal liability when others who created the problem refuse to come forward.

I know from my experience with Superfund toxic-waste sites that there are some bad guys out there. Ever since this program began, responsible corporations willing to pay their fair share have been calling for more vigorous enforcement from the federal government.

If we don't allow our government to act, or if it can't act, then we'll all be in a pickle. We'll have more direct action like the current "Big Green" initiative in California, which would impose strictures that are either unenforceable or economically disastrous. Worse still, the

California initiative would create an environmental czar with authority outside the normal channels of government—someone like Tom Hayden who would attend summits at Sundance, Utah, and whose title would be the People's Deputy on the Supreme Committee on Ecology and the Rational Use of the State of California's Resources.

And that is why the fourth rule may be the most important: Companies should build environmental thinking into every phase of their product production and distribution, from research and design to development, packaging, and disposal. Environmental managers need to get out of the basements and into the front offices. The finest engineering and business talent must hard-wire environmental considerations into the basic framework of businesses.

When environmental thinking becomes an integral part of top management's strategic and product planning, several things will happen. First, your jobs will become a lot easier. Johnson & Johnson's ability to respond to Tylenol's contamination quickly and surely required a coordinated business and public relations effort. That effort flowed from a corporate culture that embodied a melding of safety and business interests.

When that integration occurs in corporations in regard to environmental issues, I wager that you will spend a lot less time in the after-the-fact cleanup and "fix-it" business and a lot more eliciting information from citizens on their expectations and needs before large projects leave the drawing board. Public relations will shift several degrees to citizen participation. And as the "public" aspect of decision making rises in corporate America, you must become a member of your company's product planning and project-siting teams.

Another change will be in the role of lawyers. The current stress on asset-protection strategies will give way to broader and more long-term economic thinking about how to react to environmental liabilities. And as executives on the business side increasingly make environmental decisions, the dominance of lawyers at environmental negotiations will give way to a mix of professionals, including public affairs specialists.

And most importantly, when corporate America invests its finest talent in the business of making environmental decisions, for example, in deciding whether it's most cost-effective to install pollution control technology at the front- or back-end, or in devising new products that don't become liabilities, environmental decision-making then will begin more consistently to improve the bottom line.

And, for good measure, he throws in an argument that must strike fear into the hearts of rapacious capitalists everywhere, namely that the most antienvironmental public policies have been the product of communist countries. I happen to love guilt-by-association rhetoric.

The proposition that environmentally based decisions are good business decisions certainly won't be true in every case. Yet Eastern Europe is the most striking evidence that ignoring environmental impact in the long run is the worst business decision.

Our long-term interest lies in strong, effective action by our government in the environment, and strong and responsible action by corporate America. No reasonable person can doubt the importance of corporations and the free-market economy in finding solutions to the pressing problems of the environment. You only have to look at the environmental desolation of Eastern Europe to realize the virtues of such institutions as private property, which provide an incentive to protect the land and natural resources. When it comes to something like the whaling industry, any smart capitalist knows that you can amortize the ships, you can amortize the harpoons, but you can't amortize the whales. Once they're gone, your business is gone.

We have learned a lot in the twenty years between Earth Days. The most important lesson is that we're all in this together. We are ready to do what's needed to protect this planet, ourselves, and future generations.

APPENDIX
2

Making a So-So Speech Better

I<small>N</small> his movie *Annie Hall*, Woody Allen says, "Those who cannot do, teach, and those who cannot teach, teach gym."

The following speech teaches the audience to be creative, but not by example. If I were listening to this speech, I'd think, "Those who can't be creative talk about it, and those who can't talk about it go into investor relations."

Still, there are important ideas here for people in the field. The boldface comments arc mine.

A Speech on Creativity in Investor Relations

The most basic job of investor relations is providing information, and most of us are pretty good at that. We know the essential facts about our companies; we know how to make those facts available to analysts and portfolio managers in convenient form; and we generally know if

175

there are misperceptions that need to be corrected. All of that is well and good.

But the most basic job of a speech is to persuade, and you'll never persuade an audience to be creative if you aren't creative yourself. The larger point of this speech is that investor relations experts have to make sure their clients stand out in a crowded field of numbers, prospectuses, and sheer propaganda. This speech needs to start with a bang.

But I want to spend a few minutes this morning talking about another part of IR that many of us forget, and that's CREATIVITY. We've become so information-oriented in this age that it's easy to concentrate on the facts and neglect to think about how those facts get PRESENTED.

The points here and in the following paragraph are well taken, but not well made. This is very basic material, so basic in fact that an audience may dismiss it. You have to state it in a way that will make them take notice.

When you formulate an investor-relations program, what do you think about? You think about whom you want to reach; you think about an agenda for the analyst meetings; you think about the annual report. But how much time do you spend on ways to make people pay attention to those things?

Most of us in this field could benefit from thinking a bit more like a product marketer. Don't distinguish "them" from "us" in a negative way. Lots of people in this audience will consider themselves to be pretty clever, too. If a packaged-goods company wants to sell a new kind of soap flake, it had better put the product in an attention-getting box. The soap is important too, of course, but no matter how well it foams or how sweet it smells, it won't matter if the consumers don't notice. **Analogies, metaphors, and examples should be vivid. The soap image is too obviously contrived and too general to stick in a listener's mind.**

Investor relations is not so different. No matter how compelling your information may be, it does no good unless people NOTICE.

The hard truth is that most companies have to do *something* to stand out from the crowd. If your company is just one of many making lookalike computers or selling a service that's widely available, then you need a way to shout for the investor's attention. You have to *stand out*. If your company is such a strange conglomeration of disparate parts that the analysts don't bother with it, then you've got to find a *creative* way to educate them, to make them pay attention to the underlying value.

Just what kind of problems lend themselves to creative solutions? Well, as I mentioned, **you are now in minute two of the speech. You have no excuse to refer back to minute one.** If there are ninety-nine other companies making the same product yours does, or if your company makes a product no one ever heard of, then you need to get attention. And chances are you won't get much attention unless you find a way to jump and shout for it— creatively. **This is now the fourth use of a variant of the word creative without a single example of what it** means. The first rule of creative writing is "show it, don't tell it." Get on with it!

My favorite example: An example at last! But why use your "favorite" first? If it's that good, everything after it will be anticlimactic. Is a telecommunications company that came up with a more effective communications system specifically for offshore oil rigs, which seldom have enough telephone capacity. To emphasize this product's importance, the company sent analysts a cylindrically shaped package with a label that said: "One way to increase your offshore telecommunications capacity." The package contained a bottle with a message inside, and the message said: "A message in a bottle is certainly inexpensive and easy . . . But reliable it is not."

A postscript hinted that more information would follow. And the next day, messengers delivered fact books on the new product to each analyst's desk. But what a dull follow-up. There has to be a better way.

I also liked the way one company recently unveiled a new liquid detergent for automatic dishwashers. The company wanted to make the point that this was no ordinary product, but, rather, an important innovation that would have significant impact on earnings. So its IR staff called business and financial editors—it could just as well have called up analysts—and told them it was treating them to lunch the next day and to be sure to hang around their desks around noontime. Then it had messengers deliver a beautiful boxed lunch, complete with real china, glass, cutlery, Perrier, and, of course, a bottle of the new dishwashing liquid—with a fact book and an 800 telephone number for questions.

To me, the idea of sending a box lunch to be eaten at the desk struck just the right tone. As I said before, "**As I said before . . .**" **You've only been talking for three minutes. If the point needs to be made again so soon, find a "creative" way of bringing it up so soon or restructure the speech to make the point powerfully once. In this case, the point is terribly important so give it the emphasis it deserves.** Analysts— members of the press too, for that matter—are conservative people. They are ALWAYS critical of meetings or gestures that are overly lavish. Sending them lunch at their desks said to them, in effect, "Look, we know you are busy people. But here's one new product that is really worthy of attention." If the box lunch had included an expensive bottle of champagne instead of Perrier, the effect would have been lost. Creative gestures in IR have to be low-key and in keeping with the basic message, or the reaction is invariably negative.

Here's another example of some attention-getting IR. "**Here's another example . . .**" **Find another way to make this transition. Also, "attention-getting" is a very weak substitute for "creative," which is, you'll now agree, overused.** A diversified chemical company was having trouble stirring interest in its stock, which happened to sell for less than ten dollars a share. Obviously, this was a stock for individuals, not institutions, but reaching the retail investor with information about a confusing conglomerate is especially difficult. If you assume that your audience doesn't know it should be creative, don't assume that anything else will be obvious. Words like "obviously" condescend to people who don't know this, and even those who understand may have to think about why it should be so. Assume nothing and explain what you mean. Besides, I'm not sure there's an obvious reason why a share price under ten dollars should be more appealing to individuals than to institutions.

So this company did something ingenious: It announced a contest for retail representatives. Don't use words like "ingenious" lightly. People who don't agree with your high opinion will think you are a dope.

The broker who came up with the most accurate prediction for the company's sales and earnings that year won a thirty-six-foot cabin cruiser. The brokers all called up their firms' research departments, of course, and they probably all got much the same information. But the contest was a brilliant way of making them pay serious attention to the company. And it couldn't have hurt to have the analysts suddenly bombarded with questions about a little stock they'd never bothered with before. That was a wonderfully creative way of screaming for attention. Okay. It was a cool idea. But after describing it as "attention-getting" and "ingenious" a critical pronouncement is excessive. Let's face it, if it weren't "wonderfully creative" you wouldn't have used it.

Creativity can be essential in breaking ground with

investors who barely know your company. This is a problem that arises all the time now, with companies trying to raise capital in different markets around the world. Globalization is a "megatrend." You should introduce it in a way that befits a large and important theme instead of as a tail to a more generic problem. There is one major obstacle in trying to interest American analysts in foreign stocks that is almost entirely an investor-relations problem. American analysts tend to suspect that British analysts will always get the first word about important financial developments concerning British companies, just as they suspect the Japanese will get first warning about developments concerning Japanese companies. Usually, those fears are justified. But GBDC, the Giant British Drug Company, found a highly creative way to cope with this. Last month, it reserved some satellite capacity and used it to hold a meeting with analysts and investors in London, New York, and Edinburgh simultaneously. And because the broadcast used the latest interactive technology, analysts in all three cities could not only hear and see the company presentation, they could also ask questions and *be seen* by the GBDC officials. **But did it work? That should be clear.**

Maybe cleverest of all was a scheme devised by Al Bumen, head of investor relations at Righton Corporation in San Francisco. Righton's main business is a little difficult for some people to grasp. It doesn't *make* anything; it *distributes* other people's products to drug store chains. Al worked long and hard at convincing institutional investors that this was a company worth following, but retail investors posed the ultimate challenge.

Here's what he did:

First, Al and his staff prepared an advertisement that ran in *Barrons*, *Forbes*, and the *Wall Street Journal*. The ad contained highlights of the company's recent performance and was aimed squarely at individuals and stockbrokers. It gave an 800 phone number and an address, so that readers could call or write for more information. And, importantly, the ads also promised to send interested investors the *names* of stockbrokers across the country who were familiar with Righton. Responses to these ads numbered about a thousand a month.

But that was only half of the Righton program. At the same time, they sent mailings to fifty-five thousand *brokers* whose names were obtained from Technimetrics. Each of those brokers got copies of the magazine ads, a schedule of when they would be published, *and* a note saying that Righton would be happy to mail that broker's name to interested investors. All the broker had to do was respond. The initial response from *that* mailing was an unbelievable four thousand! Needless to say, that's a list of brokers with whom Righton maintains rigorous communications. Because of annual project updates, there are now some seven thousand retail reps across the country who—to one degree or another—really DO follow Righton Corporation. **A whole lot of numbers here, some of which are not as obviously astounding as the writer thinks.**

Incidentally, that IR campaign also apparently attracted significant interest from professional money managers; institutional holdings in the stock rose from 52 to 58 percent, while the number of individual shareholders rose 25 percent. How could the numbers of institutional and individual shareholders both rise at the same time? Simple: increased turnover and trading volume. In other words, better market liquidity—another big plus for the stock.

You also want to call attention to your stock, of course, when you have good news. You want to amplify it, and make sure as many people know about it as possible. One major packaged-goods company wanted analysts to know that a new toothpaste it was introducing in this country *already* had the largest share of market *worldwide*. It sent each analyst a basket filled with tubes of toothpaste from each country where it sold—with printing in all the different countries' languages. Inside the basket was a map showing where the product was made and where it was marketed. **Don't belabor the obvious. It will dull audience attention for the more important idea to follow.**

There's a problem, though, with calling extra attention to a company when the news is good: it means you are going to get criticized if you don't go to equal lengths to communicate when the news is *bad*. Is there any place for creativity when the news you've got to report is bad? In one sense, there is no place at all. When the news is bad, an IR program has to stick to fundamentals—cover all the bases, minimize the surprises and make sure the company gets *its* story out. You don't want your investors drawing all their conclusions from newspaper accounts.

But there are creative (**creative!**) ways to go about that task. When one company finally had to announce its first disappointing earnings quarter in a long, long time, it notified twenty-three analysts who covered the company a *week* in advance that there would be a conference call just after the earnings release in which they were invited to participate.

One large equipment manufacturer had to announce that it was closing five plants in five different communities. **This being a negative example, there's a good reason not to mention the company by name. But describing it as an "equipment manufacturer" is too general. Choose nonidentifying details that sound meaningful.**

This was a significant piece of financial news, but it was also very bad news for the five communities involved and, of course, for the employees who were losing their jobs. The problem here was timing. The company could *not* break the news to employees first without breaking the law, and it could not break the news to the financial world first without seeming heartless.

The solution: First, the company trained managers at each of the five plant sites to deal with employees, the press and local government officials. Then it set up an analysts' meeting and timed press releases so that everything happened at once.

To me, creativity (**creativity!**) in investor relations

doesn't always mean *gimmicks*. This is a crucial point. It should have been made much earlier. Often, the most critical IR problem is simply explaining a complex development so that investors can appreciate its importance. A computer company had two major new product enhancements of equal importance to its bottom line, but both the benefits and the marketing strategy behind these new gizmos were, admittedly, hard to comprehend. "Enhancements" is vague enough. Are these enhancements hardware or software? Does software qualify as a "gizmo" or does it fall under the category of "bells and whistles?" Describing abstractions with other abstractions is deadly. If you have to use jargon, use jargon that is specific to the field. So much so, in fact, that a mass meeting with the analysts would have been pointless. Too dismissive. If you can't lead the audience through the reasoning that leads to a judgment like this, say something like "wouldn't have done the subject justice."

So instead, the company rented hotel rooms in New York for two days, and set up one-on-one appointments with each sell-side analyst—six of them a day. The analysts did *not* have an easy time of it. *Each* of them met with *two* separate product teams from the company who explained the new enhancements and answered questions; then each analyst met with the company's financial team to go over the potential effects on the balance sheet. *Finally*, each analyst was seated at a computer terminal for a *total* demonstration of how the new products worked. That was a creative (**creative!**) approach to a difficult educational problem. **But did it work? If you're going to describe the process, describe the result, perhaps in the form of a documented response to the overall presentation.** "or, in the words of one analyst, 'gee whiz.' "

Is there ever such a thing as *too much* creativity? There definitely is. **"There definitely is." You don't need a declarative sentence to give a one-word answer, unless it's a great sentence.** Let me tell you about the chairman of an Israeli company who was planning a road show here to introduce analysts to a complicated new product. Now, this was a product that took a lot of explaining, and, to be honest **"to be honest" is one of those phrases that could lead an audience to conclude that you might not have been telling the truth all along** the Israeli's English was pretty trying as well. To make matters worse, the chairman refused all manner of suggestions from his IR counsel as to how he might improve the presentation.

The executive did make one concession, though. Midway through his long, tedious discussion of the new product, he flashed a slide before his audience showing a roomful of haggard executives sitting around a conference table looking exhausted. It was a silly little touch meant to emphasize how long and hard the company had labored. Unfortunately, the roomful of analysts identified strongly with the people in the slide and began to laugh; our Israeli lost them completely. **This anecdote is a muddle of precision and generalization. Many details are omitted [with good reason], and those that are** included only call attention to the facts that aren't there. Those that are included will reflect badly on the speaker himself. E.g., why specify the speaker's nationality? This could happen to any arrogant CEO, which is like saying any CEO, since humility is not usually part of the job specs for people who head large companies. Beyond that, it could happen to any nonnative English speaker. Last, it raises the stereotype of the arrogant Israeli. This guy made a mistake. He wasn't fated to do so by his nationality. So choose your details carefully.

I bring this up in order to point out that being creative doesn't mean being ridiculous. It should *enhance* the basic message that the company needs to convey. Otherwise, it has no place at all. So when you're thinking creatively about an IR program, there are four questions you ought to keep asking: First, is the creative gesture you're about to make in good taste? Second, is it consistent with the character of your company? Third, does it reinforce the message you want to convey? And finally, is it creativity merely for the sake of creativity? If the honest answer to that last question is 'yes'—don't do it! Remember, the whole point of an investor relations program is to *add* to the information flow, not detract from it.

The following list of examples isn't bad. But it should be compressed and compressed some more. Economy is important.

But creativity is a lot more than just attention-getting stunts. What if you represent a foreign company and you want to overcome individual investors' fears about buying international stocks? Why not hold some seminars on international markets for brokers and investors in some major cities?

What if you work for a small company that's not very well known in this country? Bob Brazil had that problem with U.S. Nuclear Family—a company that gets 70 percent of its revenues from Japan. He held a contest for shareholders and stockbrokers, asking them to estimate the company's revenues and earnings for a six month period. The prize—a trip to Japan to tour company operations and to sightsee.

What if your company produced copper? No matter how many facts you supplied about your mining costs and operations, investors would still be suspicious about future *demand* for your product. Would you consider holding a seminar with representatives from the auto world and capital goods producers to *talk* about that issue?

What if you represent one of the auto makers and you wanted shareholders to feel some excitement about your new line of cars? Why not invite them to a preview before the public and invite them to bring along friends? OR, if you're a food company, why not put discount coupons in your annual report to encourage shareholders to get to know your products?

Would you like your employees to take more interest in the company's well being? How about producing an annual report for children or developing a board game about the company, so that workers can go home at night and talk about their employer with pride.

All of these things are simple examples of presenting

information in ways that appeal to the investors you want to reach. *That* kind of creativity is essential to almost any effective IR program. The information we have to give investors is our most important product. But it's also important to convey some basic messages about the company and its future. Creativity is really a matter of packaging those messages, along with the facts, so that investors will want to find out what's inside.

APPENDIX
3

Second Draft

T HE following is a second draft of the above speech, done according to some of the criticisms.

Analysts Are People, Too

Analysts are people, too. In our field, investor relations, we may sometimes operate on the assumption that they sit in their cubicles, looking for cracks in our numbers through which they can drive armored personnel carriers, and so drive down the price of our shares. But while the most basic job of investor relations is providing information, it's not the only job. "Just the facts, ma'am, nothing but the facts" may be good enough for Sgt. Joe Friday, but this isn't *Dragnet*, and investor relations isn't police work.

We know the essential facts about our companies; we know how to make those facts available to analysts and portfolio managers in convenient form; and we generally know if there are misperceptions that need to be corrected. All well and good.

But there's something to be said for how all that information is presented. Numbers crunching can be mind-numbing, even for people who like it. I'm not crazy about it myself, which may be one reason I'm on this side of the discussion and not the other one. To give our clients the treatment they deserve, we have to make sure their companies stand out from other annual reports, prospectuses, and financials that flow across analysts' desks.

Dull investor relations probably never killed a company that had good products, and exciting IR never saved a company with bad ones. But bad IR takes its toll in the form of excessive share-price volatility, because too few people own the stock. Or because there isn't the right mix of individual and institutional shareholders. Weak share prices can raise the cost of company debt. Over the long haul, this capital drag takes its toll on the real business of any company—giving its customers better products, and better service.

So to get a fair stock-market valuation, you have to make sure that your message gets through to the investment community. But how? When you plot an investor-relations strategy, what do you think about? Whom you want to reach; agendas for the analyst meetings; the annual report. These are the obvious things. And when you consider that the SEC is lurking just offstage, it's obviously very important.

But analysts aren't just creatures of the stock market. They're human. They're consumers. Very discriminating consumers, but consumers nevertheless. And we have to create brand credibility for our client companies, because it will be very important not just when there's good news to tell, but, as you'll see later, when there's bad news as well.

Well, enough of this theory. How does it work in practice?

One favorite of mine was a company that came up with a more effective communications system specifically for offshore oil rigs, which seldom have enough telephone capacity. The company sent analysts a cylindrically shaped package with a label that said: "One way to increase your offshore telecommunications capacity." The package contained a bottle with a message inside that read: "A message in a bottle is certainly inexpensive and easy. . . . But reliable it is not."

A postscript hinted that more information would follow. The next day, messengers delivered fact books on the new product to each analyst's desk. By the time they arrived, the analysts were ready to read them.

Not every problem lends itself to such a neat solution. You can't get much more specialized than telecommunications for seafaring roughnecks. That kind of detail makes for surgically precise messages. But as the problem grows less distinct, there's more need to be creative.

Say your company makes lookalike computers. Or sells a service that's widely available. In such cases, you have an even more compelling need to shout for the investor's attention. Yet solutions may be harder to find.

Remember, analysts are people, too. Their time is

limited. A new liquid detergent for automatic dish-washers may seem like a pretty ho-hum product in an already crowded field. Then, too, consider that analysts as a class are unlikely to have an instinctive appreciation for the fine points of dishwashing.

It's a tough nut to crack. But one company found a hook that could appeal to these people in terms they could relate to. This was no ordinary product, but rather an important innovation that would have significant impact on earnings. So the IR staff called not only analysts but business and financial editors as well. They told them they were being treated to lunch the next day and to be sure to be at their desks around noontime.

At the appointed hour, messengers delivered a beautiful box lunch, complete with real china, glass, cutlery, Perrier, and, of course, a bottle of the new dishwashing liquid— with a fact book and an 800 telephone number for questions.

To me, sending lunch to be eaten at their desks struck just the right combination of showbiz and practicality. Analysts and members of the press may like their expense accounts as well as the next guy. But when it comes to the companies they're following, extravagance is a dirty word. They are always critical of gestures that are too lavish. Sending them lunch at their desks said to them, in effect, "Look, we know you are busy people. But here's one new product that is really worthy of attention." If the box lunch had included an expensive bottle of champagne instead of Perrier, the effect might have been lost in the afternoon haze. The china, glass, and cutlery were a must. After all, someone would have to wash the dishes after they finished eating.

Creative gestures in IR have to be low-key and in keeping with the basic message, or the reaction is invariably negative.

A new entry to a crowded field isn't the only problem a company can encounter. Some corporations are such strange conglomerations of disparate parts that the analysts don't bother with them. Or they may analyze these companies in terms that they feel comfortable with, but that don't do justice to its unique strengths. Or they might simply not pay enough attention. Then you've got to find ways to educate them, to make them pay attention to the underlying value.

A diversified chemical company was having trouble stirring interest in its stock, which happened to sell for less than ten dollars a share. One of the barriers to a higher price was that its shares were held mostly by institutions, which knew value when they saw it. Raising awareness among individual investors was seen as a way of raising the price as well. But reaching the retail investor with information about a confusing conglomerate is especially difficult.

The way to reach individual investors isn't just a matter of talking to analysts. It's also a matter of reaching their brokers. So the company announced a contest for retail brokers. The one who came up with the most accurate prediction for the company's sales and earnings that year would win a thirty-six-foot cabin cruiser.

The brokers all called up their firms' research departments. The analysts were suddenly bombarded with questions about an unfamiliar stock. The stock went up. The one question that remains is whether the winning broker ever invited his analytic staff out on the boat.

One of the most thorough schemes was devised by a company that distributes products to drug-store chains. This was not the most evocative company that ever went public. It could never claim to reach out and touch someone, or be the heartbeat of America. Still, it was very successful in the marketplace, and wanted its due from Wall Street as well. After a long effort to convince institutional investors that this was a company worth following, they turned to retail investors.

First, they prepared an advertisement that ran in *Barrons*, *Forbes*, and the *Wall Street Journal*. It highlighted the company's recent performance and gave an 800 phone number and an address so that readers could call or write for more information. And, importantly, the ads also promised to send interested investors the names of stockbrokers across the country who were familiar with the company. Responses to these ads numbered about a thousand a month.

But that was only half of it. At the same time, they sent mailings to fifty-five thousand brokers. Each broker got copies of the magazine ads, a schedule of when they would be published, and a note saying that the company would be happy to mail that broker's name to interested investors. All the broker had to do was respond. The initial response from the mailing was four thousand. It has now grown to seven thousand brokers who, because of annual project updates, are avid followers of the stock.

Because of this campaign, interest in the stock has risen among both individual and institutional investors. Institutional holdings have risen from 52 to 58 percent, while the number of individual shareholders rose 25 percent.

One of the dominant trends in business these days is the increase of global competition. Companies that once relied on their own domestic markets are now looking around the world both to sell their products and also to manufacture them. And in a world where a single national market for goods is no longer sufficient, a single national capital market is no longer enough either.

The cultural problems of operating in a global capital environment are no less than the marketing problems. Analysts are ethnocentric. American analysts think that British analysts will always get the first word on important financial developments about British companies. They think that the Japanese will get first warning on developments concerning Japanese companies.

Not that Americans are any more suspicious than anyone else. Brits, the Japanese, and everyone else are all just as skeptical as we are.

And they are probably right. But there are ways of coping.

Giant British Drug Company reserved some satellite time and used it to hold a meeting with analysts and investors in London, New York, and Edinburgh simultaneously. The broadcast used the latest interactive technology, so analysts in all three cities could ask GBDC management whatever questions they wanted, face to face.

One major packaged-goods company wanted analysts to know that a new toothpaste it was introducing in the United States already had the largest share of market worldwide. It sent each analyst a basket of tubes of toothpaste from each country where it sold—with printing in all the different countries' languages. Each basket also held a map showing where the product was made and where it was marketed.

You naturally want to call attention to your stock when you have good news. There's a problem with making too much noise in good times. When things go wrong, your investors may notice the silence.

The challenge to a creative investor-relations program is even greater when the news is bad than when it is good. You have to cover the fundamentals, minimize the surprises, and make sure that if the company's version is better than the publicity, the story gets out. You don't want your investors drawing all their conclusions from newspaper accounts.

Analysts and investors come to rely on you. They want to believe you. If you are candid with them even in bad times, you will remain credible when things improve.

When one company finally had to announce its first disappointing earnings quarter in a long, long time, it invited twenty-three analysts who covered the company a week in advance to participate in a conference call just after the earnings release.

A construction equipment manufacturer had to announce closings of five plants in five different communities. This was a significant piece of financial news not only on Wall Street; it was also very bad news for the five communities and, of course, for the employees who were losing their jobs. Timing was critical. The company could not break the news to employees first without breaking the law. And it could not break the news to the financial world first without seeming heartless.

The solution: First, the company trained managers at each of the five plant sites to deal with employees, the press, and local government officials. Then it set up an analysts' meeting and timed press releases so that everything happened at once.

As cases like this make clear, creativity in investor relations doesn't mean gimmicks. But gimmick-free IR isn't only useful in crisis management. Sometimes, it simply means explaining a complex development so that investors can appreciate its importance.

A computer company had two major new product enhancements of equal importance to its bottom line. But they realized that the benefits and the marketing strategy would have to be seen to be understood. So instead of, say, holding a mass meeting with the analysts, the company rented hotel rooms in New York for two days. Then they put together a kind of Manhattan version of Outward Bound. Six sell-side analysts a day went one-on-one with two separate product teams from the company which explained the new enhancements and answered questions; then each analyst met with the company's financial team to go over the potential effects on the balance sheet. Finally, each analyst was seated at a computer terminal for a total demonstration of how the new products worked. It worked. As one analyst put it, "Exhausting but enlightening."

Is there ever such a thing as being too clever for your own good? In a word, yes. The chairman of a foreign company was planning a road show to introduce Wall Street analysts to a complicated new product. It took a lot of explaining, a problem complicated by the chairman's limited grasp of English. For good measure, he refused suggestions from his IR counsel as to how he might improve the presentation.

To add a headache to an upset stomach, he tried to display a bit of the common touch. Midway through his long, tedious discussion of the new product, the CEO flashed a slide of some haggard executives sitting around a conference table. He meant to emphasize how long and hard the company had labored. Unfortunately, the analysts identified strongly with the people in the slide and began to laugh. Whatever faults this fellow had in his presentation, it was an honest effort. Yet he ended up playing the buffoon.

I bring this up to make two points. One, CEOs should always listen to their IR counsel. As long as there are executives like this one, people like us will always have a job.

But seriously, creative investor relations should be sublime. If there's a chance of becoming ridiculous, don't do it. It should enhance the basic message that the company needs to convey. Otherwise, it has no place at all. Better to stick to the numbers.

So when you're thinking creatively about an IR program, there are four questions you ought to ask: First, is the creative gesture in good taste? Second, is it consistent with the character of your company? Third, does it reinforce the message you want to convey? And finally, is it creativity merely for the sake of creativity? If the honest answer to that last question is "yes"—don't do it! Remember, the whole point of an investor-relations program is to reinforce the information flow, not detract from it.

I would say, however, that the right answer is the creative answer more often than not. If you represent a foreign company and you want to overcome individual investors' fears about buying international stocks, why not hold some seminars on international markets for brokers and investors in major cities?

What if your company produced copper? All the facts about mining costs and operations wouldn't allay investor suspicions about future demand. How about holding a seminar with representatives from the auto world and capital-goods producers to discuss it?

If you represent one of the auto makers, how about stirring up excitement about your new line of cars by inviting them and their friends to preview the new line? If you're a food company, why not put discount coupons in your annual report to encourage shareholders to try your products?

And remember, there are other constituencies that can benefit from the same kind of thinking. Want your employees to put their money in a stock investment plan? How about producing an annual report for their children, or developing a board game about the company, so that workers can go home at night and think about their employer as more than just a meal ticket?

All of these things are simple examples of presenting information in ways that appeal to the investors you want to reach. That kind of creativity is essential to almost any effective IR program.

The information we have to give investors should be as good as the products we sell.

Ultimately, of course, the message is only as good as those products. The greatest IR program in the world won't save a company that can't compete in the marketplace. But communicating effectively with the investment community is an essential part of the overall message. The payoff in terms of capital costs can make the difference between a company that stays in the forefront of the industry worldwide, and just another player in a highly competitive global economy.

In the last analysis, creative investor relations costs no more than just reporting the facts, but the rewards are substantial. The real difference will be on the bottom line.

APPENDIX
4

*A Good Speech, and Why It Is
Good*

Let's see. The elements of a good speech are a strong message, delivered by an authoritative speaker with great conviction; internal logic bolstered by facts; and with pertinent quotations that impart historic perspective and cultural plausibility, good, strong language, and self-confident humor. The following speech fits the bill on every score.

The Business of America
A.W. Clausen,
Chairman, Bank America
Santa Clara, Ca.
May 19, 1988

Calvin Coolidge once said that the business of America is business. That was a long time ago.

Today, the business of America is corporate raiding, white knights, golden parachutes, greenmail, and junk bonds. **Coolidge's line is a real old saw, but it is used** in a fresh way, being brought up to date by the second sentence.

Franklin D. Roosevelt said it best. "We have always known that heedless self-interest was bad morals," he said in his second inaugural address, "we now know it's bad economics. And bad for society." **Roosevelt's observation provides apt perspective, having been made when the U.S. and the rest of the world were mired in the Depression, the hangover from the wild party of the Roaring Twenties. This kind of perspective is ominous.**

I believe our current preoccupation with mergers is bad economics. And bad for society. **Not bad for a big-time banker from California to cast himself with the hero of the New Deal. Strong thesis. Adds social dimension to notion of good business according to Coolidge.**

When you ponder that the value of merger and acquisition transactions was $167.5 billion last year, or about 23 percent of gross private domestic investment, you can understand why we're having trouble competing in world markets. These investments produce no new wealth. They rather fit former RCA chairman Robert Sarnoff's definition of finance: the passing of money from ·hand to hand until it disappears. **Good quote, and it would be a good quote if Karl Marx had said it. Sarnoff is no Marx, and it makes the point much stronger.**

Takeovers force management into going for the short-term. The logic is, keep earnings high. Keep the stock price high. Maybe the raiders will pick on someone else. Raiders, who cast themselves as the shareholder's protector, therefore, are the shareholder's biggest problem because management that's preoccupied in foiling a takeover is distracted from plans that ensure long-term survival and prosperity.

Sometimes this preoccupation repeals the canons of good operating procedure. For example, any elementary finance book will tell you that the more liquid your company is, the less risk. But these days, being liquid is risky. Liquid assets draw raiders like stagnant pools draw mosquitoes. **Gross imagery. Equating raiders with mosquitoes is no accident. Elegant, and very damning.**

In the nation's largest nonoil merger, General Electric picked up RCA for sixty-three dollars a share. But RCA had cash on hand equaling ten dollars a share, which GE used to leverage the deal.

Liquidity attracts the raider, or suitor, as in the case of GE, who can expect to finance part of the takeover from the acquired company's own coffers. Therefore companies that want to avoid being taken over often squander their cash. Sometimes they make investments totally alien to their purpose.

Cash is often converted into assets for which there is little market and little earnings potential. These make the target company less attractive, and therefore, less likely to be taken over.

The trend away from ready cash is already manifest in

the decline in the quick ratio—the ratio of liquid assets to current liabilities—over the last several decades.

In the late forties, when I began my career, the quick ratio for manufacturing was 1.07. By the late fifties, it dropped to .57, and now it's around .15. The lower the ratio, the greater the likelihood of default or bankruptcy.

Ratios, however, have denominators as well as numerators. And the increase in short-term debt used to finance takeovers also contributes to the decline of this ratio.

An even better barometer of the increased risk is the ratio of short-term corporate debt to overall corporate debt. A company with a high ratio will be under greater strain in servicing the debt. And, predictably, this ratio has been increasing, rising from .23 in the early 1970s to about .35 today.

The most flagrant form of takeover leverage is the junk bond. Junk bonds were once the province of junk companies, firms deemed shaky by the various rating agencies and suitable for only the boldest investors. A decade ago, less than $1.5 billion of these lowly securities was outstanding. Today there's more than $142 billion of junk out there, or about one-fifth of the totality of corporate bonds.

The new-issue market for junk bonds has grown geometrically over the last decade, from $1.5 billion in 1978 to $7.4 billion in 1983, to $48 billion in 1986. **Good numbers. Very dramatic increases. You can't lump these statistics with lies and damned lies.**

What does all this high-yield leverage portend for the economy? Well, last year a Los Angeles consulting firm identified thirty-six companies as vulnerable to insolvency as a result of junk-bond leverage. The firm concluded that about 5.5 percent of all the junk bonds outstanding is vulnerable to default, which is three times the historical rate of default for publicly traded junk bonds.

More than 80 percent of these bonds have never endured the test of a general economic downturn or a sustained period of rising interest rates. As Pete V. Domenici, the Republican senator from New Mexico who chaired the Senate Budget Committee, noted, "Comparing today's explosion of junk bonds with their use in the late 1970s is like comparing World War II with the Civil War simply because gunpowder was used in both."

Junk bonds can be issued not only to acquire outside companies, but also to finance leveraged buyouts. This highly leveraged way of taking a company private is an effective antitakeover maneuver but can be damaging to balance sheets and prudent operations.

The margin of error in these deals is so small that any setback can be disastrous. Fruehauf, a trailer maker, took on $1.4 billion of debt when it completed its LBO in 1986 to thwart a takeover. Debt as a percentage of assets immediately shot from 35 percent to 85 percent. What no one saw was that the assets Fruehauf planned to sell would fetch less than the planned prices, and that sales would not grow as projected. Fruehauf has cut its debt to $780 million, and it's down to 75 percent of assets. But the company has had to part with more assets than anticipated, including its trailer operations and most of its European division.

Before companies take on the burden of excessive debt, they should consider the wisdom of Miss Piggy, "Never eat more than you can lift." **If you have a chance to quote Miss Piggy with this kind of effect, do it. No one will wonder if your speaker is spending too much time watching *Sesame Street*.**

Corporations still have much to learn about living with debt loads once thought foolhardy. Junk bonds, takeover madness, and takeover fears have forced us to suspend our belief that too much debt is dangerous. But, for reasons painfully driven home by folklore, the dread of debt is part of our psyches. Right now, attending a bit more seriously to the voice within might save a few companies from going over the edge. **Beginning with this paragraph, the speech wields conventional wisdom like the Ten Commandments.**

Although the United States has yet to experience the fallout from what one wag called the "explosion of atomic bonds" **(swell pun)** history does afford a few examples. The most noteworthy occurred in the early twenties in Europe. Hugo Stinnes, a German industrialist every bit the equal of Andrew Carnegie or Harold Geneen, built an enormous corporate edifice on the foundation of junk debt. During the Weimar inflation, his assets grew faster than an elephant pup. But then old Hugo died, the inflation abated, and his heirs kept on borrowing and buying. The Stinnes bankruptcy—and it was one of many in Germany at that time—was like Penn Central, Equity Funding, and W. T. Grant rolled into one. Reaches back into the collective consciousness to show how merger frenzy is at odds with real American values.

Clearly, in America, companies with 16 percent paper in a 4 percent inflation environment are asking for trouble. Even a modest downturn could lead to a number of failures. Time will tell. But unfortunately, if the bell tolls, it tolls for you and me. That's the nature of the economy.

By borrowing heavily to buy control, of course, a corporate raider can use the target company's own assets to finance the deal. Once in charge, the new owner can sell off pieces of the company and divert cash flow to pay off acquisition loans. That's how the leverage pays off. When the original gap between the stock-market value and the split-up value of the acquired company is large— and the raider's equity investment negligible—the returns on investment are just short of miraculous. Some companies taken private in the bear market of 1980–81 and resold to the public in 1983 returned ten dollars for every one dollar of equity invested.

The reason this sort of arbitrage exists, of course, is because companies are valued as "going concerns" and priced on current earnings. The raiders, however, value them on the basis of liquidation value.

The wisdom of Graham and Dodd, the gurus of securities analysis, doesn't figure in these transactions. Rather, it's the economics of the Chicago stockyards. A cow is not an animal that produces milk and cheese. Rather, it's something to be eviscerated, hacked up, and sold piecemeal. In short, you have to kill the cow. **More repugnant imagery, bringing to mind Upton Sinclair and *The Jungle*.** And often the raiders end up killing the corporations, eviscerating them of valuable employees who pay taxes, and maybe also killing the town where the company was headquartered.

Despite the baleful consequences of takeovers, many thoughtful people argue that they are good for the economy. Their argument is reminiscent of William Nye's comment that Wagner's music is better than it sounds. **Wagner quote elegantly undercuts the raiders' most high-minded argument.**

The claim is that shareholders benefit when stock prices are bid up, superannuated workers fired, and underperforming assets sold. I could agree that shareholders do benefit from these things. But that's hardly the pattern in most hostile takeovers.

I think the real test of the takeover is how the shareholders of the acquiring company fare. The conglomerates of the sixties certainly didn't do very well. And overall, the results are disappointing. Michael Seely, an authority on mergers with Investors Access Corporation states that, "In the past decade only one-third of all mergers have enriched the acquirer's shareholders, one-third have been a wash, and one-third have ended up costing investors money—sometimes lots of it."

Even if hostile takeovers did benefit the shareholders—

and the benefits are quite short-lived—they are not good for the economy, and certainly not good for society.

Most Americans in the workforce are members of organizations—be they blue-collar workers, middle managers, or even chairmen of boards. Americans are a cooperative lot. We'll pull together during hard times. We'll rise to a challenge. But one thing we won't stand for is being treated like chattels. We've fought too many wars to allow that to happen. We've routed too many tyrants to allow our hard-won security to be threatened by outsiders, people not even a part of the organizations we've devoted our lives to. *Tarte tatin* **(French apple pie) and motherhood. Brooks Brothers and blue collars are on the barricades together.**

We can make adjustments to hard times for the good of the company. But this, of course, is not the rationale for the hostile purchase of human organizations and subsequent sale of vital parts of the business. That rationale has nothing to do with human enterprise and everything to do with enriching someone who has nothing to do with the enterprise and who, admittedly, is interested only in looting it. By enriching themselves, they're impoverishing society. These parvenus are simply a bunch of crumbs held together by dough.

Chapter 11 of the U.S. Bankruptcy laws asserts that the rights of the creditor are not absolute, and that before proceeding to the drastic step of liquidation, the firm has the right to reorganize itself into a viable concern.

The spirit of this law might be summed up in saying that a company is worth more living than dead. Not necessarily worth more to the creditors or shareholders—although, in the long run, that's usually the case—but worth more to society.

Allowing our institutions to be chopped up and sold on the auction block, and our devoted employees to be discharged like peons, is to transgress the spirit of our laws and values of our civilization.

Unless the business of America is business, we'll be out of business. **Neat symmetry. Returns to Coolidge, plays neatly off the original sentiment.**

About the Author

Henry Ehrlich writes speeches for a major financial institution in New York City. He is the author of *A Time to Search*, the stories of adopted people who went looking for the families that gave them up. He is married with three children.

Selected Readings

Allen, Steve. *How to Make a Speech*, McGraw-Hill, New York, 1986.

Copeland, Lewis and Lamm, Lawrence. *The World's Greatest Speeches*, Dover, New York, rev. 1973.

Filson, Brent. *Executive Speeches: 51 CEOs Tell You How to Do Yours*, Williamstown Publishing, Williamstown, Massachusetts, 1991.

Leeds, Dorothy. *PowerSpeak*, Prentice-Hall, New York, 1988.

Noonan, Peggy. *What I Saw at the Revolution*, Random House, New York, 1990.

The Oxford Book of Legal Anecdotes, Sutherland, James Runcieman (ed.), Oxford University Press, Oxford and New York, 1975.

The Oxford Book of Literary Anecdotes, Gilbert, Michael (ed.), Oxford University Press, Oxford and New York, 1986.

The Oxford Book of Military Anecdotes, Hastings, Max (ed.), Oxford University Press, Oxford and New York, 1985.

"Rhetoric," *Encyclopedia Britannica*, Vol. 15, pp. 798–805, Chicago, rev. 1984.

Safire, William. *The New York Times*, annual critiques of president's State of the Union Address.

Sarnoff, Dorothy. *Speech Can Change Your Life*, Doubleday, New York, 1970.

SELECTED READINGS

Sparks, Will. *Who Spoke to the President Last?* Norton, New York, 1971.

Speechwriter's Newsletter (weekly), Lawrence Ragan Communications, Inc., 407 South Dearborn St., Suite 1360, Chicago, Illinois 60605–9974.

Vital Speeches of the Day (semimonthly), City News Publishing Co., P.O. Box 1247, Mt. Pleasant, South Carolina.

Wriston, Walter B. *Risk and Other Four Letter Words*, Harper and Row, New York, 1984.